ALBERT HADLEY

ALBERT HADLEY

THE STORY OF AMERICA'S PREEMINENT INTERIOR DESIGNER

ADAM LEWIS

RIZZOLI
NEW YORK

To Betsy

A. H.

To Thom

A. L.

First published in the United States of America in 2005
by Rizzoli International Publications, Inc.
300 Park Avenue South
New York, NY 10010
www.rizzoliusa.com

2007 2008 / 10 9 8 7 6 5 4

Designed by Abigail Sturges

Printed in China

ISBN-13: 978-0-8478-2742-8
ISBN-10: 0-8478-2742-9

Library of Congress Cataloging-in-Publication Data

Lewis, Adam.
Albert Hadley : The story of America's preeminent
interior designer / by Adam Lewis.—1st US ed.
p. cm.
Includes bibliographical references and index.
ISBN 0-8478-2742-9 (cloth : alk. paper)
1. Hadley, Albert. 2. Interior decorators—United
States—Biography. I. Title.
NK2004.3.H33L49 2005
747'.092--dc22

2005007724

*The fabrics and wallpapers used throughout
this book were designed by Albert Hadley.*

HALF TITLE
*Albert Hadley student design project,
Parsons School of Design, 1947*

TITLE
Niles

DEDICATION
*Albert Hadley tablescape, small photo of
Elsie de Wolfe, large photo of Betsy Hadley
by Wilbur Pippin*

Contents

8   Foreword by Annette de la Renta

10   Acknowledgments

12   Introduction

20   *Fireworks*

28   *Nashville*

42   *Sail Away*

52   *The Capital of the World*

62   *Pieces of the Puzzle*

72   *Moving Up and Out*

98   *A Fine Romance*

116   *The People Who Make It Happen*

202   *A Decorator Is Never Alone*

212   *Albert Hadley, Inc.*

262   Catalogue Raisonné

268   Bibliography

269   Index

271   Photography Credits

272   About the Author

Foreword

by Annette de la Renta

Albert is a "True North" in our world—a gentleman of enormous integrity and modesty. Never once, in the more than forty years I've known him, have I heard him say a single unkind word about anyone—or anyone's work. He is so polite that even if he thinks you've had a major lapse in judgement, he'll never ask, "Have you lost your mind?" At most, you might get a quiet, "Are you absolutely sure?"

Like Billy Baldwin and later, Bill Blass, he has a completely American, architectural approach, and a perfect sense of scale. Sister created a chintz-and-Dark Harbor coziness with grand English touches. Albert injected what was spare and modern and architectural into that look, which is what made the team so effective—he brought Parish-Hadley into a younger, more "real" world. And though he may have picked up some of Sister's softness, his mantra remains "simplify." He instinctively knows what's important and eschews the pompous. Where lesser talents seem always to want to add, Albert subtracts.

We've worked on a lot of projects together over the years, but the two favorites will always be our house in Katonah, New York, and another in Dark Harbor, Maine. Looking back on the Katonah experience, I think that Albert must have been living on Tylenol because I gave him such headaches. He was at his most minimal and I was at my most excessive.

Oakleaf Trellis

It was in the very early seventies and I was having a reaction against all that chrome and the safety of beige and white. Unfortunately for Albert, I decided I wanted to go in a vaguely Victorian, Madeleine Castaing direction, and somehow he made it work wonderfully. There was a lot of laughter—his wry sense of humor saved the day.

In Dark Harbor, he stenciled the floors, painted all the wicker white or black, and had big upholstered furniture everywhere. The walls were covered with brown wrapping paper and hung with the elephant Audubon prints. The exterior was the deepest brown/black with white trim—it may sound dreadful but it was wonderful.

What must be said about Albert is that he has extraordinary affection for and generosity towards young people, and he is always willing to help them get started, as both assistants and clients. It is remarkable that so many talented people learned from working with Albert, and he is constantly enthusiastic in teaching and helping. With Albert, not everything has to cost a fortune—he understands the chic of putting something inexpensive into the mix. I revere his eye, I rely on his always being the voice of calm and reason, and I admire the enormously important contributions he has made to American decorating. But I love him for the kind and thoughtful man he is.

Acknowledgments

My gratitude begins with Albert Hadley. This book could not have been written without his collaboration and support. It is not easy for a person to trust someone with the intimate details of his or her history, as is required in writing a biography. In addition to the close examination of the most private aspects of the subject's life, the process also requires a great commitment of time. Throughout the course of this work—including years of research and untold hours of tape-recorded interviews—Albert has been the consummate gentleman. I am grateful that he gave me the opportunity to write his story and that I have arrived at the end of the project knowing that Albert Hadley will be forever a treasured friend.

Betsy Hadley, a true southern lady, has graciously provided important information about her brother and their family. Every member of Albert Hadley's staff—Nancy Porter, his personal secretary; Carol Cavalizzo, the office manager of Albert Hadley, Inc.; José Santos, the company driver; each of his three assisting designers, Harry Heissman, Peter Lentz, and most especially Britton Smith—have given enormous assistance in the creation of this book. To each of them and Betsy Hadley, I am grateful.

Dotted Shell

My appreciation goes to Annette de la Renta, who wrote the foreword; Helen Pratt, my literary agent, who never stopped believing that this book would be published; Kathleen Jayes, my editor, and Charles Miers, my publisher, who both gave me their immeasurable support; Abigail Sturges, who designed this book; John T. Hill, who provided original photographs and the photography that was necessary for production; Ray Roberts, my friend and mentor, who is always either cheering me on or pulling tight on my rein; Harry Hinson, who provided a font of information on the American interior design community; Willoughby Newton and Claudia Thomas, who were my readers; and to Duane Hampton; Betty Sherrill, chairman of McMillen, Inc., and Ethel Smith and Luis Rey, also of McMillen, Inc.; Elizabeth Broman and Stephen Van Dyk at the Cooper-Hewitt, National Design Museum, Smithsonian Institution; Stan Friedman and Michael Stier at Condé Nast Publications; and Inge Heckel, president of the New York School of Interior Design. If there is anyone I have forgotten to thank, please forgive me.

Finally to Thom Chu, my companion, who is always generous with his help and indefatigable in his patience, and to whom I offer my unending gratitude.

Introduction

Albert Hadley and I first met in 1996 while I was writing the biography of Van Day Truex, the third Dean of New York City's Parsons School of Design and former Design Director for Tiffany & Co. Hadley and Truex had been professional colleagues and enjoyed a friendship that began in 1947 when Hadley was a student at Parsons. Truex was then head of the school. Immediately after Hadley graduated, Truex offered him a position on the interior design faculty. He taught there for five years before opening his own design firm in 1955. Hadley's natural bent for teaching and his encyclopedic knowledge of interior design was ever present in our many discussions. From my initial meeting with him and throughout the writing of the Truex book, he was indispensable in helping to order the information I collected from the myriad interviews I had with people who knew Truex. Frequently I would share with Hadley that one person I interviewed told me something that conflicted with information I had gained from an earlier interview. Hadley was quick to sort out the details and get to the core of the truth. Having been an interior designer for more than fifty years, Hadley has personally known every American designer of note, and, down to the most minute detail, he is thoroughly familiar with the history of the decorating trade.

Kimono

When I called to schedule our first appointment, Hadley invited me to come for cocktails at his apartment. Aware of his reputation as the dean of American interior design and having seen his work featured in the *New York Times* and leading shelter magazines, I was anxious about our meeting. I knew that the information I gained from him would be valuable to the success of the Truex biography. As with any interview, one hopes that the right questions will be asked. There was no reason for me to have been apprehensive. I would discover that Albert Hadley, with his many accomplishments and august reputation, is a remarkably personable, witty, and genuinely kind man. I would discover that his quote in *House Beautiful*, "Life is all about manners. Nothing else matters," is much more than an expression about deportment. For Hadley it is a creed.

Arriving at his building, the doorman said that Mr. Hadley was expecting me and to go right up. As the elevator opened, I could see Hadley peering from behind the door. As the door opened further, his face projected a ruddy complexion, bushy eyebrows, dark horn-rimmed Le Corbusier–style glasses with amber tinted lenses and a broad, welcoming smile. He said, "I'm Albert Hadley. Come in. I want to hear all about your book." His demeanor, the tenor of his voice, and his warm handshake gave the immediate impression that he was genuinely interested in me and my work.

Taking off my coat in the foyer, Hadley said that he would hang it in the coat closet. I offered to put it on a nearby chair and he responded, "Oh, no, no I would rather hang it up," which he did. This was my introduction to the orderly world of Albert Hadley. There was nothing pretentious about what he did or the way in which it was done. A sense of appropriateness and suitability is inherent in Hadley's nature. A coat closet is for coats. A chair is for sitting. On all of my subsequent visits, and there were many, the ritual of his hanging up my coat never varied.

Hadley was wearing what I came to think of as his uniform: a black cashmere turtleneck sweater, dark gray flannel trousers, and well-worn, polished L.L. Bean moccasins. In every photograph I had ever seen of him, he had been wearing this same outfit. On occasion he would add a black and gray herringbone wool sport coat. The one part of his attire that photographs had not shown was his fire engine red socks.

As we walked through the living room, I could not resist commenting on the hologram paper squares that covered the ceiling and the insert of mirror that forms a border separating the ceiling from the wall and the floor from the wall. "Experiments," said Hadley. "My whole apartment is an experiment. The mirror is to give the illusion that the walls float. Ceilings must always be considered. They are the most neglected surface in a room." Like the wall of the entrance hall, the walls of the hall into the study were painted a brilliant red and highly varnished. The ceiling in the study, where we sat, was painted deep black luster.

In the study and in the living room there were many Van Day Truex drawings—some hanging on the walls, some on the floor leaning against the wall, and some propped on shelves or table tops. In the hall I recognized Douglas Abdel's sculpture *Naexa-Alkyad* that Truex bought a few weeks before his death in 1979. On the console in the library, Hadley had the two small Fazzini sculptures of diving boys that Truex bought in Italy and on the wall above was one of Truex's most important paintings of two oversized bull head sculptures in an Italian garden. While these were all outward and visible signs of Hadley's close ties with Truex, the bond they shared would be revealed more clearly in Hadley's anecdotes.

A natural raconteur, Hadley wove into his Truex stories amusing reminiscences about Billy Baldwin, who was Truex's closest confidant. While Hadley was almost twenty years younger than either Truex or Baldwin, the three men were frequently together, they held one another in highest regard, and admired one another's talent and eye. All of this was supported by their keen wit and bon mots. Baldwin once said to Hadley, "You know, Albert, Van thinks he has perfect taste, whatever that means." Their mutual admiration formed the foundation for a unique tripartite liaison in the interior design community. Evidence of Truex's respect for Hadley was exhibited in 1967 when he asked him to be his successor as the design director at Tiffany & Co. Eleven years later, in 1978, Walter Hoving, president of Tiffany's, again offered Hadley the position at Truex's urging. On both occasions Hadley refused.

One day when we were scheduled to meet, Hadley called to say he had invited the interior designer Bunny Williams, the fashion illustrator Jay Hyde

Crawford, and Alan Campbell, a noted fabric designer who died in 2001, all of whom had known Truex, to join us. This was characteristic of the help that Hadley gave to me throughout the writing of the Truex book. Often when I would arrive he would have on the coffee table some articles from his files and books that he had taken from his collection. He would go over each article and single out passages or chapters from the books, saying, "Feel free to borrow these. They will help you to better understand Van's world."

As our conversations and discussions allowed me to know more about Van Day Truex, they also gave me insight into Albert Hadley. As he became more comfortable with me and my questions, he was more open to talk about his own life. While he may be the most modest person I have ever known, as he recounted stories about his career and his list of distinguished clients, I always knew that I was with one of the most important men in the history of interior design.

Each time I was with him I realized more fully why noted editors and writers often referred to him as a "genius of design." Hearing about his vast accomplishments, it was clear to me that his story had to be told to a wider audience. While *Parish-Hadley, Sixty Years of American Design* is a handsome record of the interior decoration done by Hadley and his former business partner, the late Sister Parish, it ends just before Mrs. Parish's death in 1994 and does not focus on Hadley's career. Since the book was published in 1995, he has gone on to a completely new venture. In 1999, he closed Parish-Hadley, Inc., and in January 2000, in his ninth decade, opened Albert Hadley, Inc. Like a great runner, he has gained a second wind, and continues to do exciting work. I knew that when I completed the Truex biography, writing Hadley's biography and assembling a complete record of his work would be my next project.

Convincing Hadley to let me write his story was not easy. While he speaks freely about his ideas and theories on design and decorating, he is cautious, if not loath, to talk about his personal life. His sense of extreme privacy made it difficult for him to reveal his inner self. This trait is readily evident in the ways he spends his time when he is not working. Days and evenings alone with his music, reading, drawing or making collages, and reworking and reviewing his files are his most enjoyed pastimes. Although he is inundated with invitations to gala art events and theater openings, extravagant charity benefits and opulent openings of major museum shows, renowned antiques shows and decorator show houses, among other media events, Hadley much prefers to spend evenings alone or with a few select friends. If he does accept an invitation to support a charity or attend a friend's art opening, he is usually the first to arrive and after a short time makes a quiet, gracious exit. Another of his proclivities is rising early to have uninterrupted time to review his work for the day. This early morning discipline and his quiet evenings alone are evidence of the deep spiritual aspect in his nature.

When I discussed the idea of a book on Albert Hadley with Helen Pratt, my literary agent, she gave me enormous encouragement which added to my enthusiasm. When I approached Hadley with the idea, he refused to consider it: "Write the book after I am dead. Then you can say

English hall chair in Hadley's Manhattan apartment. The "H" on the wall was embroidered by his grandmother for his grandfather's silk top hat.

what you want. I do not want to get involved." While he is known for his open-mindedness and love of experimentation, Hadley is fiercely firm when he makes up his mind. Try as I would to get him to think positively about the project, he would not budge. Finally, at one of the book-signing parties for the Truex book, Helen came up to me and said, "Albert has just told me that he is going to let you write his story." Typical of Hadley, he left the party early. As he made his exit, he came by the table where I was signing books and said, "Helen has some news for you. I hope you will be pleased." Of course I was, and my response was, "We start tomorrow."

The two years of writing and reviewing hours of taped interviews have all been a joy for me. Getting to know Albert Hadley has been a rewarding experience. In this book Hadley's own words are set in italic type or, in some instances, defined with quotation marks. I hope that I have succeeded in letting him tell his own story.

Fireworks

O n November 11, 1920, in Springfield, Tennessee, Albert Livingston Hadley, Jr., son of Albert Livingston Hadley and Lois Meguiar Hadley, was born into one of the state's most historically important families. His grandmother, Mathilda Wade Hadley, was a direct descendent of John Donelson, who had been one of the original settlers of Nashville. His great-grandfather, Dr. John Livingston Hadley, a descendant of Irish Quakers who came to America in 1712, was born in North Carolina in 1788. His great-grandfather's father, John Hadley, married Margaret Livingston, a relative of Robert Livingston, who helped to draft the Declaration of Independence. John Livingston Hadley, their only child, entered the University of North Carolina, completed the curriculum there, and studied medicine with Dr. Benjamin Rush in Philadelphia. Having received his medical degree from the University of Pennsylvania, young Dr. Hadley served as an army surgeon in the War of 1812. After the war ended he went to Tennessee, where he married his first cousin Amelia Hadley. The newlyweds lived in Nashville until 1820, when they moved to Hadley's Bend and built Vaucluse, one of the most imposing and beautiful plantation houses in the state.

Hadley's mother and father took great relish in their family's contributions to the early history of Tennessee. They had equal pride in their immediate family and children. Bolstered by his parents' reminiscences of his arrival, Hadley delights in telling about his birth day and the Armistice celebration that took place that evening.

On the second anniversary of the Armistice that ended World War I, sometime between midnight and dawn, I was born in my parents' home. That evening, my father, Bert Hadley, who was a tall, imposing, handsome man, held me in his arms as he looked out on the antics of his neighbors and gazed into the night sky that was ablaze with light. Dazzling fireworks exploding over the town celebrated the end of the Great War. The cool autumn air was electric with excitement and the sounds of music, singing, and laughter. While my mother, Lois, rested in bed, my father shared with her what he could see from the window. Throngs of people were gathered in the town square. Some were dancing. The narrow roads that radiated out from the town into the countryside were filled with people on horseback and in horse-drawn buggies and wagons coming in for the festivities.

My mother and father had their own cause for celebration—a new son. Their first child, also a son, born about a year before, had lived for

Hadley with his mother

only a few hours. The sadness that had over-taken them after the child's death was now lifted. On many occasions Mother told me that my father was as proud as any parent could be when I was born. Father said that I was an alert baby and my eyes blinked in unison with the brilliant flashing fireworks. To this day I believe that I can remember that night and the brilliant spectacular lights from exploding fireworks. Whether I can remember this or not is unimportant. I have always loved fireworks and still do. They mark the begin-ning of my life, which has been colored by fantasy and sup-ported by a world of dreams. These two, fantasy and dreams, have been my mainstay in a world that is not always perfect.

In recalling his early years, Hadley displays a remarkable, somewhat uncanny memory for details of the houses where he lived. He vividly remembers the colors and the decorative details of the rooms and their furnishings.

Soon after I was born, my father sold his buggy and farm implement business in Springfield, and we moved to the outskirts of Nashville. Both of my parents had grown up in the countryside near Nashville. Our house, a compact cottage that sat squarely in a green grassy yard, was on the street that marked the end of the streetcar line. A fence of gleaming silver wire formed the boundary between our yard and the street. Newly planted umbrella trees flanked the walk that led from the front gate to the house. The three wide entrance steps ended on an even wider porch. As a young bride, Mother accepted the way that my father had furnished his house in Springfield, but now the time had come for her to use her talent and furnish the new house according to her taste. She painted all of the rooms one of three colors—white, pale blue, or pale gray.

The living room was small but bright and cheerful. There was a fire-place and tall wide windows. When closed at night, simple clear yellow cretonne curtains added a note of cheer to the pale gray walls and white trim. The furnishings were sufficient but sparse and arranged for comfort and use. There was a very pretty patterned rug and an assortment of dark wood tables and chairs. The highlight of the room was a glorious Tiffany electric lamp that had been a wedding present to my parents. The tall bronze base was worked in a stylistic form that vaguely suggested the trunk of a tree. On the dome-shaped glass shade was the scene of a landscape that was colored by an exuberant sunset. This one important electric light stood in the center of a large oval book table that was placed in the middle of the room. When the light was on and the sunset glowed I suppose it was easy to understand Mother's choice of pale gray for the walls.

The only other room in the house I remember with any clarity was my parents' bedroom. It was painted pale blue with soft ivory trim and furnished with a beautiful, painted new bedroom suite. The furniture was classical in silhouette with an innovative detail of woven cane work set into panels on all of the major pieces. The brass hardware was fashioned like swags of flower garlands. There was a bed, a dresser, a high chest, and a few small tables and chairs. The rich ivory color of the paint was a dramatic contrast to all of the dark wood furniture that I had known up until then. I thought this was the most beautiful room on earth and maybe even heaven.

One morning when I had been left alone in the bedroom, I was sitting on the floor, across from the footboard of the bed, working with my crayons. The caning that was set into the wide panel of the high footboard was woven in a pattern that resembled pale little circles. I began filling in the circles, using a different color for each one. I had yet to learn the sophistication and chic of ivory and its many close color associates so I thought the effect that I was creating was a great improvement.

Hadley with his maternal grandmother, Maggie Meguiar

When Mother returned and saw what I had done, she quickly put a stop to my artistic endeavors.

There were few, if any, children of my age in this new neighborhood. I amused myself with coloring books, adventures with make-believe friends, my fox terrier, named Night, and my fat black cat, named Day.

I thought that our next-door neighbor, a widow known simply as Mrs. Epps, was a nifty dresser. I often talked about the brilliantly cut, sparkling red glass beads that she frequently wore. I was enamored by her beads and I longed to have some, not to wear but to hold and see the fractured scarlet light through them.

Some days before Christmas when my father asked me what I wanted from Santa Claus, the only answer I could think of was red glass beads. One evening soon after I had made my request, my father said that he heard some noises on the roof and thought it might be Santa Claus. Filled with excitement, I followed Mother's suggestion and dashed to the window to see what was going on. The moment my back was turned, my father tossed a string of red glass beads onto the stone hearth of the fireplace. Hearing the tinkle of the beads, I was convinced that they had slipped out of Santa's pack and fallen down the chimney. I was one happy little boy and the beads became my talisman. My absolute favorite gift from

Santa that year was a complete Indian suit consisting of leggings, an elabo-rately beaded and fringed jacket made of synthetic doe skin, matching moc-casins, and best of all, a tall multicolored, feathered Indian chief's bonnet.

For me, riding the streetcar in and out of town was an excitement not to be believed. The rhythmic sound of the heavy iron wheels rumbling along on the tracks was intoxicating. Another of my great delights was an evening trip to the drugstore for an ice cream cone. It was always a mystery to me that a place of pure pleasure should have such an awful name—drugstore. Most of the walls of the drugstore were covered with gleaming mirrors trimmed with polished chrome. On one of the mirrored walls there were glass shelves that held tall, clear glass canisters filled with bright-colored candy. For me this sparkling display was the wonder of wonders. Each time we went to the drugstore, I was completely happy.

When I was about three, my maternal grandfather died. The day of his funeral was bitter cold with icy wind. I was spared going to the funeral service and stayed with a cousin at Broadmoor, my grandparents' farm. Stretched out before the fire, with a new box of crayons and a fash-ion magazine, I added color to the illustrations. There were few, if any, colored pictures in magazines in those days.

When the family returned from the cemetery I looked up to see my grandmother swathed in black from head to toe. A black crepe veil was attached to her Queen Mary–style hat by two dazzling jet hat pins. The veil covered her face and fell almost to the hem of her black-as-the-ace-of-spades, crepe de chine dress. After removing her gloves with her exquisitely long, tapering fingers, in an elegant gesture she lifted the veil over the hat so that it fell in soft folds about her shoulders. Watching her, I thought that my heart would stop beating. She was the most beautiful thing I had ever seen. I bounced up and presented her with one of my col-ored drawings. When she saw it, her chiseled, calm face became radiant with smiles of amusement, and she broke into deep-throated laughter. My gift counteracted any tendency toward tears of mourning.

Hadley is adamant in his belief that good interior decoration is determined by the architectural elements that form the design project. He frequently refers to "the bones" of a house or an apartment, which he says must always be the designer's first consideration. Beyond concepts that can be learned, these principles are inherent in his nature. Hadley was five years old when he spent a year at Broadmoor. His ability to recall with vivid accuracy the details of this house and the other houses he lived in before he was six, is evidence of his acute awareness of design at an early age.

For reasons I have never known, we left our Nashville house, my land of enchantment, and went to live with my widowed grandmother and her unmarried daughter, Mary. Grandmother's home, Broad-moor, was located five and a half miles outside of Nashville on the Gallatin Pike.

Soon after their first child, Mary Hillard Meguiar, was born in 1893, my grandfather, Alexander Franklin Meguiar, and his wife, Maggie

Hillard moved from Franklin, Kentucky, to a farm outside of Nashville. They called their new farm Broadmoor. Having left the management of the McElvain-Meguiar Bank and Trust Company to his former business partner, grandfather was starting a new life for his family. On October 1, 1894, their second child, my mother, Elizabeth Lois Meguiar, was born. From the beginning, Broadmoor was her home.

Originally Broadmoor had been a simple mid-nineteenth-century house consisting of two large rooms separated by a wide, generous hall on both the main floor and the floor above. Extending beyond the room on the right side of the hall, on the ground floor, was a long wing of smaller rooms, which included the kitchen, pantry, and a storage area. Before my grandfather bought the house, a two-story wing had been added to the front. It was only as wide as the center hall but accommodated a parlor and a stairway hall. The second story consisted of a single bedroom.

When we moved to Broadmoor it was a working farm, so there were chickens, cows, pigs, and horses for both work and pleasure. Here I learned to ride with my father. The two things I remember most vividly about our winter there were my dog, Night, dying and my having a terrible bout with double pneumonia.

Grandmother was delighted to have all of her family around her, under one roof. Broadmoor was her farm, this was her house, and we were her family. She managed the lot of us with the polished dexterity of a three-ring circus master. Aunt Mary was happy that her sister had come home, and she took me on as her charge. Of course, I was pleased to be the focus of my mother's, grandmother's, and aunt's attention and care.

The only person who wasn't happy at Broadmoor was my father. His life was dominated by women. During our first winter there, my grandmother assigned the care and management of the farm to him, and she and Aunt Mary left for Florida. This only added to his restlessness.

In the spring when Grandmother and Aunt Mary returned from Florida, my father had bought some acreage of heavily wooded land not more than a mile from Broadmoor. Here he found his longed for, special place. He named the place In the Woods.

Father worked from a simple, no-nonsense plan for the house. Everything was thought out and carefully executed. While he enlisted some help from local carpenters, Father did most of the work himself and produced a strong, well-built structure. It was a small clapboard house with a shingle roof. A large, beautifully-worked stone chimney rose through the center giving a sense of honest quality and stability to the modest house. The narrow road that wound its way from the lane above the house ended in a small turn around at the front entrance. A little covered porch protected the big plank front door that opened directly into a marvelous large living room. If style is the result of form following function, then In the Woods was a house of sturdy American style. This place was Father's prized creation. It was the house that he built with his own hands for his family.

My parents quickly made headway on the house. The big room that stretched across the length of the house was centered by the impressive

The Meguiar homestead,
Franklin, Kentucky

front door made of vertical planks that were stained the black-brown color of creosote, the substance used to coat telephone poles. Centered on the walls on either side of the front door were windows set low to the floor and reaching almost to the height of the wide plank ceiling. Windows were also centered on the walls at each end of the room. Opposite the front door was a stone fireplace that was practically large enough for a man to walk into. The room was a place of light and dark; the walls were a pale warm gray that related to the color of the stone chimney; the floor was stained the same black-brown color that was on the door; the wooden ceiling, the other doors, and the trim were natural wood.

The few pieces of furniture that had been in the house in town were comfortably displayed here. The electric Tiffany lamp was missing from the center table. This house, like Broadmoor, had no electricity or other modern conveniences. When the colorful simple little cretonne curtains were drawn across the windows at night, the firelight, candles, and oil lamps cast entrancing light and shadows.

The door on the right side of the fireplace opened into the kitchen, which had a pantry and storage room. The door on the left opened into the bedroom, which was painted a soft atmospheric blue. It was the perfect setting for mother's painted bedroom furniture.

In 1926 the family moved back to Nashville, after living at In the Woods for slightly more than a year. Hadley was nearly six years old and it was time for him to begin school. He had spent most of his life in the company of adults, farm animals and pets.

Nashville

Soon after the Hadley family moved back to Nashville, Lois Hadley gave birth to a daughter, Betty Ann. While there was considerable difference in their ages, from the beginning Albert was devoted to his baby sister, and Betsy, as he called her, grew to have deep affection and admiration for her big brother. According to Hadley, there was one grievous problem when they returned to Nashville: the house that his parents bought.

While I was only six years old, I already had strong opinions about houses and rooms. No one could persuade me that the new house wasn't ugly. It was constructed of a new building material—cast cement—to look like rustic stone. It had no charm whatsoever. The fake stone marks the beginning of my lifelong dislike for shams.

At least in the summer the entire facade of the porch was covered with morning glory vines. The vines made the porch cool, and the blue color of the morning glory flowers was a revelation. I suddenly saw blue everywhere—in Mother's willowware, in the cobalt finger bowls that were lined up on the serving table. Red had been my first color—the red beads. My new color was blue. Deep drifts of four o'clock were planted on the north side of the house. As their name implies, every afternoon at four they opened to reveal a blossom that was brilliant pink, a color that Elsa Schiaparelli would later call "shocking." Immediately this intense pink was added to my color palette.

The most important thing that happened to me while we lived in the ugly house was hearing the news that Lindbergh had landed in Paris. In those days we only had a crystal radio set that we listened to with earphones. As the news was coming in and being repeated over and over, the earphones were passed around the family. As I sat hearing the announcer tell about the landing, the crowds, and the excitement of the event, I could imagine that I was there. The news of Lindbergh transported me. This is why I have always loved listening to the radio. The experience allows the listener to imagine anything.

After two years in what Hadley refers to as the "ugly house," the family moved again. This time they moved into a new house that was built on property that had been a part of Broadmoor.

Grandmother sold Broadmoor to a land developer and the farm was divided into building lots. Mother and Father bought one of the largest lots

Hadley with his sister, Betsy

that had room for a garden. At the same time that we moved from the ugly house into mother's dream house, a big farm-machinery firm offered my father a job as a salesman. Always a country boy at heart, he seized the chance to spend his days with farmers, driving around in his yellow coupe.

Mother found the plans for the new house in a home furnishings magazine. Constructed of bricks that were the color of hand-churned butter, the house had a shingle roof. The exterior white trim was accented by the black-green color of the shutters. The steep gables resembled houses I had seen in a storybook about Hansel and Gretel. I was then nine years old and interested in every aspect of the house—the construction and the finishing details. I was forever trying to get Mother to go a bit further with her decorating schemes. One of my triumphs was getting her to paint her ivory bedroom furniture a bright apple green.

The interior plastering and painting was being done by a crew of highly enthusiastic Italians. Their Mediterranean spirit and breathtakingly beautiful work was best used in the living room. After Mother showed them the fabric for the curtains, which was a dull green cloth woven with vines and leaves and shot through with gold thread that highlighted the design, the painters had a field day. They first painted the walls a creamy mustard color. After the paint was dry they worked their magic with wads of cheesecloth that had been dipped in a soft green paint—smearing, patting, and rubbing. The translucent shimmering color made the room fairly glow. This was my first lesson in interior decorating.

Not only was Hadley interested in the building of the house, he vividly recalls every detail of his mother's choice of fabrics and colors and his involvement in the work. His memories also display a prodigious ability to compare and contrast his mother's decorating choices with those of her mother.

The fabrics and colors that Mother chose for the living room were reminiscent of the parlor in which she had grown up at Broadmoor. The year that we lived there with Grandmother and Aunt Mary I thought that the parlor had a magical, mysterious air, like a bejeweled cave. In true Victorian style, a tall gold-framed mirror hung over the black marble mantel and gilded pelmets were above the windows. The floral pattern of the wallpaper, printed in cream, tan, brown, and moss green, was embossed with gold. A small Turkish rug was laid on top of smooth straw matting that was put down in strips. For the highly carved, ornamental, upholstered parlor furniture and for the curtains, which Grandmother made herself, she used a medium moss green-patterned brocatelle that was highlighted with a gold thread.

The fabrics that she used on the other furniture, various stools, and cushions were chosen without any attempt to conform to a color scheme. There was a consistency in Grandmother's daring madness that produced a certain continuity, and the room had an air of comfort, quality, and casual elegance. When the dark louvered shutters were opened, usually only on Sunday, the light that flickered in through the heavy lace undercurtains created romantic shadows. In the evening when the oil lamp, on the center marble-topped table, was burning, the glow of its pink glass shade and the lighted candles on the mantel and the piano filled the room with a soft flickering light. I have never forgotten the allure of the parlor at Broadmoor.

One of my favorite pastimes was going with Mother and her friends on what they called "antiquing" days. She and one or two other ladies and I would take off for the country in her gleaming blue sedan. Mother would stop at any house that looked promising, knock on the door, and ask the people if they had anything they wished to sell. More often than not they did have things they no longer wanted or used and were glad to get the money. If Mother bought a piece of furniture or something that was too big to get into the car, my father would go out on the weekend and bring back her purchases in his truck. To this day I love rescuing things from people's attics or basements. I enjoy using what my clients already have. As a decorating scheme is planned, I always leave room for filling in here and there with their own things. When it is appropriate I will upgrade or rework the items.

Going to the Presbyterian Church occupied much of the Hadley family's free time. They went to morning and evening services on Sunday and attended Wednesday-evening prayer meetings. Soon after his high school graduation, Hadley became a member of the Junior Deacons. He remembers living according to "The Good Book" and being an obedient son.

If the doors of the Woodland Street Presbyterian Church were open, our family was there!

Afternoon automobile rides in the country were a favorite pastime of the Hadley family. With his wife and son and daughter, Bert Hadley loved to ride through the countryside outside of Nashville that had been his boyhood home. The land, defined by a wide horseshoe formation in the Cumberland River, was known as Hadley's Bend. Bert enjoyed telling and retelling stories of his family and Vaucluse, the home his grandparents, John and Amelia Hadley, built at Hadley's Bend. While John and Amelia were staunch Presbyterians, parties, dances, and fox hunts were a part of their life at Vaucluse. President Andrew Jackson's land, on which he built his home The Hermitage, was adjacent to that of the Hadleys. The president and his wife, Rachel, were among John and Amelia Hadley's closest friends.

Late in 1917, the nearly six thousand acres that comprised Hadley's Bend were acquired by the federal government for the construction of the world's largest black powder mill. Within six months the mill, Old Hickory Smokeless Powder Works, was in operation. Having been displaced, the Hadleys of Hadley's Bend were forced to start over in surrounding communities. A local newspaper sympathetically reporting the family's plight, said "How sad it must make [the Hadleys] feel to leave the homes where they were born and have lived such a happy life. But room must be made for the great powder plant and there is no alternative, they must go, and going, see their homes pulled to the ground and their crops destroyed."

The powder plant closed after the Armistice was signed. It had been in operation less than one year. The land was then sold to the Nashville Industrial Corporation and subsequently to the DuPont Company, which built facilities for the manufacturing of rayon. In 1924 Vaucluse was demolished to allow expansion of the rayon factory. The original Hadley family cemetery is all that is left to mark the presence of the distinguished family that lived at Hadley's Bend.

One of my father's many stories about Vaucluse concerned a pair of eighteenth-century brass andirons that his grandfather brought from North Carolina. According to family lore, the andirons were too big for any of the fireplaces in Vaucluse, so they were thrown into a rubble heap somewhere on the property. Each time we were there I made it my mission to search for the missing andirons. They were never found.

Another of Hadley's father's tales of Vaucluse was the story about the Andrew Jackson wallpaper. Supposedly, the French wallpaper used in the entrance hall of Vaucluse was ordered by President Jackson for his home, The Hermitage. The ship bringing the paper got off course and was extremely late getting to America. By the time the wallpaper finally arrived, the President had made another selection for The Hermitage and sold the paper made in Paris to his good friend and neighbor, John Hadley.

By the time I knew Hadley's Bend, the DuPont rayon factory was there. It was so enormous that locally it was known as Rayon City. My uncle, Howard Hadley, was employed by the DuPont Company, and often he would bring me a roll of cellophane, which was a by-product of rayon. Talk about excitement! That was me with a roll of the new, magical cellophane.

FOLLOWING PAGES
Fashion paper dolls Hadley designed for his sister, Betsy

Hadley fashion drawing,
"Frightened by Dali," 1931

My early years in school were uneventful. I didn't like to go to school and was a terrible student. I was much happier at home with my make-believe friends, my drawings, and our pets, especially my new dog Trixie, and our horses. I loved riding bareback. From my earliest years Aunt Mary also gave me her old copies of Vogue *and* House & Garden. *I devoured them. In* Vogue *I first read about surrealism and was fascinated by the strange images and paintings done by Giorgio de Chirico, René Magritte, and Yves Tanguy. When I was about thirteen, I started buying my own copies of the magazines, keeping me more up to date.*

Having spent the first six years of his life isolated from the company of other children, Hadley had a difficult time mixing with his peers. There is no indication that his parents found this unusual and were seemingly content for him to remain within the close confines of the immediate family.

Fashion

Tuffed Evening
wrap in PeaCock
Blue + Lemon Yello
Satin

Jon Thornwood

Early Hadley fashion drawing, 1935

On occasion he would be in the company of other aunts and uncles as well as cousins, who were children of his own generation, but he describes these gatherings as less than pleasant. Certainly they were not occasions that he happily anticipated.

Quite honestly, I was a loner. I have been a loner all of my life. If it sounds like I had a sad life growing up, I did not. I was often alone but never lonely. While I don't remember ever having a close friend, I did play with a neighbor, Russell Spotswood, who was about my age. Russell, Betsy, and I put on plays that I directed.

My parents and I frequently went to the movies. Art Deco was then the rage in Hollywood, and I thought it was simply grand. The movie stars back then were really stars. We had Greta Garbo, Joan Crawford, Katharine Hepburn, Cary Grant, Clark Gable, Gary Cooper, Fred Astaire, and Ginger Rogers. In those days all movies were in black and white.

Today I still like black-and-white movies because you can imagine any color for anything you see—the sets, the interiors, the costumes.

In the evenings, our family listened to the radio. We now had a big cabinet radio in the living room where we sat in rapt attention as we heard programs like "Little Orphan Annie" and "Amos and Andy." I have always liked the fact that I can imagine places, settings, interiors, and the way people look when I listen to the radio.

Many of the things that we take for granted today came into common use during my early years. Electric lights, indoor plumbing, automobiles, talking motion pictures, and air travel all came along as I was growing up. They were wonderful years of adventure and invention. Even though I grew up with the age of air travel, it would be a long time before I had my first plane ride, but I loved to imagine being on a plane and the thrill of being high above the clouds.

In these early years, as his artistic talent developed, Hadley spoke freely of a desire to live in the glamorous world of New York City. Both his talent and his ambitions for the glittering life of Manhattan were fostered by Hollywood movies and sophisticated magazines like *Vogue, Harper's Bazaar,* and *House & Garden.* The writings of two women, Elsie de Wolfe and Emily Post, further nurtured his yearnings.

In addition to my drawings of houses and interiors, I loved to do fashion drawings and design the dresses and hats for my models. When Gladys Lanier, a friend of the family, came to visit, she would engage me in discussions about my drawings and things that interested me. She encouraged me, and always ended our conversations with "Albert, go for it!" Mrs. Lanier made me feel good about myself and said that she was sure that one day I would live and work in New York City. One day when she came to see Mother, she brought me a copy of Elsie de Wolfe's The House in Good Taste. *This and Emily Post's* Etiquette: The Blue Book of Social Usage *were my favorite books. First published in 1922, Mrs. Post's book was about a civilized way of life that was not much different from the*

Albert Livingston Hadley

way my family lived. As I read and reread her often humorous but realistic advice on dining and entertaining, I could imagine that I was experiencing the situations she described.

After my elementary years in school, my horizons became broader. I took speech lessons and drawing lessons. I will never forget the day that our teacher, Mrs. Edwards, taught me to see negative space. We were sketching at the Parthenon, a full-scale replica of the Athenian original, which was built in Nashville in 1897 to celebrate the Tennessee Centennial. Mrs. Edwards instructed the class not to draw the columns but instead to look at and draw the spaces between the columns. For me, this was a whole new way of seeing.

That same year, Miss Jennie Mae McQuidy, my English teacher, selected me to represent our school in the county declamation or speech competition. I won first prize. In physical edu-

cation classes, I was referred to as the runt of the litter. Extremely small, I was not equipped for competitive athletics. The compromise was to assign me to dramatic arts. I wasn't interested in acting, but I enjoyed designing sets and painting scenery. Best of all for me, I was out of physical education, which I hated.

After I finished the ninth grade at the Isaac Litton School, a public school across the pike from where we lived, my parents, for reasons unknown to me, decided to send me to the Wallace School. It was the most prestigious private boys' school in Nashville, located in Belle Meade on the opposite side of town from where we lived. I shall never forget the evening when the headmaster came to our house for my interview. He talked not only to me but to mother and father as well. As he was leaving he

Lois Hadley

told my parents that he was sure there was a place for me at the Wallace School. Being there was the most distressful year of my life. All of the students, except me, were clothes-conscious, handsome, athletic young men from rich West End families. I was not one of them, nor did I want to be. Every hour I spent at the Wallace School I was miserable. When the year was over, I had not passed a single course—except spelling. It was back to Isaac Litton, where I had to repeat the tenth grade.

The final years at Isaac Litton I did very well. I wasn't an honors student but I held my own. I was allowed to take advanced drafting and architectural drawing. For a brief time I thought that I would like to be an architect, but my mathematical abilities were not up to the academic requirements. I did especially well in art, dramatics, and speech.

The summer between my junior and senior years I got a job as a salesman at Bradford's, one of Nashville's leading furniture stores. I gave my customers advice on how they could use their purchases in their *homes. My advice came from my avid devotion to the dictums of* House Beautiful, House & Garden, *and* Vogue. *From these magazines I learned about William Pahlmann, who was head of the decorating department at Lord & Taylor, and other leading New York interior designers. During my last years of high school I took drawing classes at the Watkins Art School in downtown Nashville.*

Because I was seven when I started elementary school and had to repeat the tenth grade, I was almost twenty years old when I graduated from high school. That summer I was at home with no plans for the future. Certainly I was not prepared to go to an academic college. There was a lot of talk about America entering the war in Europe and most of the men my age wondered if we would be drafted for military service.

One of my most vivid memories of this period of my life happened at the Tennessee State Fair. As my family and I walked through the great exhibition pavilion, the Paul Whiteman orchestra was above the crowd on a bandstand playing "Rhapsody in Blue." The music was being broadcast through gigantic speakers. Suddenly it stopped and an announcement came over the public address system that Hitler had invaded Poland. Everyone in the pavilion stood in stunned silence. I knew very little about Hitler, Nazi Germany, or Poland. I did know that this announcement was an omen of something big that was about to happen. I knew that whatever it was would dramatically change my life.

Early one morning, a week or so after hearing the announcement at the fair, Mother came into my room and said, quite firmly, "Wake up. Get dressed. You're going to Peabody." That day I entered the freshman class at George Peabody College of Art and Music. Peabody later became a part of Vanderbilt University. The courses I elected to study focused on art and design. One of my teachers, Miss Sobotka, told me that one of her former students, William Crandall, was a decorator in New York. She said she was sure he came back to Nashville once a year to visit his family. When he came that year I arranged to meet with him. He was my first contact with a real New York decorator. That was the highlight of my first year at Peabody.

One day, for a reason I can't remember, mother met me at Peabody. As we were walking across the campus, several people said to me "Hi, Jon," or maybe "Hello, Jon." Mother wanted to know why people were calling me "Jon." I was caught. I had to tell her that I signed all of my fashion drawings "Jon Albert." At the time, I was fascinated with anything that had to do with fashion. In my twenty-one years I had seen women go from long hair piled on top of their heads and long dresses that came down around their ankles to short skirts and bobbed hair. In Vogue *I had read about Chanel and Schiaparelli and their revolutionary designs. At the same time I was well aware that boys weren't supposed to be interested in women's fashions or costumes. At least in Nashville they weren't. To avoid being derided for one of my most enjoyable pastimes, fashion design and illustrations, I signed all of my drawings "Jon Albert." Mother was not amused by my alias, but she offered no criticism. She always told me, "Albert, be yourself."*

When my second year at Peabody ended in June 1941, I had no intention of returning and got a job as a salesman at Period Furniture Company. Five years before, when I was sixteen, I had made it my business to visit the showroom of A. Herbert Rodgers, the most prestigious decorating firm in the South. Mr. Rodgers's studio and workrooms were on West End Avenue, directly across the street from the Period Furniture Company, in the most fashionable section of Nashville. A part of Mr. Rodgers's renown came from his architectural expertise and daring use of bold colors. Having served in the army in France during World War I, he also had a great flair with French design and decoration. Meeting Mr. Rodgers and seeing his glamorous shop was a turning point in my life; I think I knew then, at that very moment, that I wanted to be an interior decorator.

Herbert Rodgers

I had been at Period Furniture Company only a few months when Mr. Rodgers offered me a job as a junior assistant in his decorating firm. When I started my new job, I did a little bit of everything—from watering the gardenia plants and ornamental trees to special tasks in the workrooms. I was exposed to every aspect of the decorating trade—upholstery, curtains, installations. In a short time I was asked to work with Mr. Rodgers on schemes and was allowed to be present when he met with clients. Accompanying him on visits to clients' houses or being sent on deliveries gave me entrée to some of the most attractive houses in Nashville. I shall never forget walking into Cheekwood, which was considered one of the most beautiful houses in the United States. Certainly it was Nashville's finest. Today it is a museum. When we delivered a small silver table to a client, I was mesmerized by the bright yellow taffeta curtains in her beautiful drawing room. This was the first time I had seen taffeta curtains and I thought they were magnificent.

Unquestionably, the training that Hadley received working with A. Herbert Rodgers ingrained in him the work ethic and principles, such as attention to detail and the belief that there is no substitute for the finest workmanship, that guide his every decision in decorating. This brief but intense exposure to excellence and refinement is reflected in Hadley's management of his firm today.

Once Mr. Rodgers assigned me the task of working on some new brass fixtures to give them a patina, but my efforts were not producing the finish that I knew he wanted. Mr. Rodgers came into the metal craft room where I was working, took off his coat, rolled up his sleeves and said, "Albert, give that blow torch to me, and I will show you how to do this correctly." This was an important lesson: A good decorator not only plans and schemes, but he also knows how the job is done. The experience of working with Mr. Rodgers was a thorough and rewarding apprenticeship. Unfortunately, it was too brief.

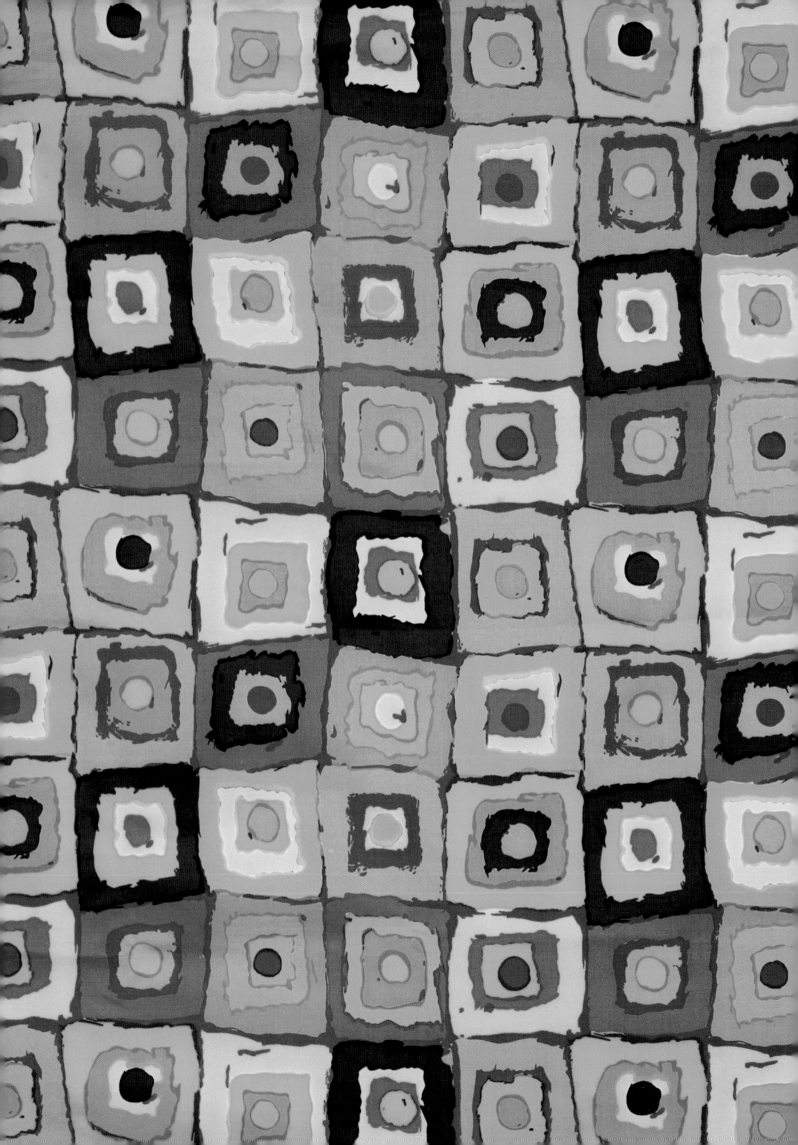

Sail Away

I n 1942, every able-bodied American man expected a draft notice from the United States Army. In early spring of that year, Hadley read that William Pahlmann, the man whom he most admired in interior design, was an officer in the army camouflage corps. Over dinner one evening, he told his parents that he had decided to volunteer for the camouflage corps, knowing that he would be drafted any day. The following morning, however, as Hadley was preparing to leave for the recruitment center, the mail arrived with his draft notice. He was ordered to immediately report to the induction center in Tullahoma, Tennessee.

It was the most difficult experience of my life. The first night that I crawled into my cot in the enormous barracks where hundreds of men were sleeping was the first time in my life that I had ever slept in a room with another person. The physical and written exams went on for three days. At the end we were told to go home and to wait for our orders for basic training. As I rode the train back to Nashville, I knew that I had to make this thing work. There was no alternative. I decided that I would pretend the whole experience was a movie—that it wasn't really happening. My idea worked. In the end, the United States Army was the best thing that ever happened to me. Immediately after basic training, which lasted only a few weeks, we were shipped out.

On the morning of May 11, 1942, we sailed into the Firth of Clyde. From Scotland, we were conveyed by train to London. I thought the experience was fabulous. Seeing England in the spring was breathtaking. All of the little villages that we passed through in this beautiful countryside were covered with waves of camouflage balloons. Our final destination was Chelmsford, a village just north of London, where we were to work with the 864th U.S. Division of Aviation Engineers building an airstrip. I was the company clerk, which meant that I was in charge of the payroll.

Even amidst the violence of war and destruction, Hadley continued to refine his eye and understanding of beauty. In blasts of bombs that brought death near, he witnessed a magnificence of light and color that titillated his imagination. The explosions he witnessed were pyrotechnics beyond his imagination.

The first night we were at the base, there was an air raid—bombs were falling, shells were exploding, there were great clouds of smoke and

Hadley with his mother and sister

brilliant flashes of light. Everyone ran from their huts to take shelter in roadside ditches. That is, everyone except me. I thought it was the most beautiful show of light I had ever seen. There was an enormous tree between where I was standing and the distant explosions. Each time a bomb fell or a shell went off, the tree became a jet black silhouette against the bursts of pink and gray and white and blue light. I was mesmerized by the beauty of it all. Suddenly, one of the men pulled me into the trench, yelling, "Get in here, Hadley. If you get killed we won't get paid."

The bombings went on all summer and into the fall, often doing damage to the work that we had just completed. I was given the additional assignment of editing a weekly battalion newsletter. Part of my job was to travel with the company chaplain to other military installations for stories and news that would interest our men. When we visited a camp for German POWs, we were astonished by the high level of morale.

When we had time off, most of the men in the battalion took the train into London. At The Rainbow Corner, the servicemen's canteen in Piccadilly, I met Lady Charles Cavendish, formerly Adele Astaire, Fred

Astaire's sister. During the war years, in both America and England, ladies from all walks of life served as hostesses at the servicemen's canteens. Lady Charles gave me a list of shops in London she thought I might enjoy visiting. One of them was the flower shop of Constance Spry. Mrs. Spry provided all of the white flowers for Lady Mendl's famous circus party in Paris just before the war. She asked me what I planned to do when the war was over. When I said I wanted to be an interior decorator, she wanted to know if I knew Elsie de Wolfe, then Lady Mendl. When I said I had never met her, Mrs. Spry told me to call Lady Mendl for an appointment and to feel free to use her name. It would be some years before I called on Lady Mendl, but Constance Spry's name opened the door for my first visit.

In November 1943, Hadley became ill with a respiratory infection and was hospitalized for several weeks. X-rays revealed that he had scars on his lungs, which were believed to have been there since his childhood bout with double pneumonia. The doctors began a series of painful treatments that involved draining and collapsing his lung. Late in the winter of 1943, the doctors ordered that he be shipped back to the United States. He went first to a military hospital on Staten Island in New York. From there he was sent to another military hospital in Memphis, Tennessee; he was honorably discharged in January 1944 and sent to a veterans hospital in Outwood, Kentucky.

I remained in the hospital for more than two years. While I was there, my first cousin, Matilda Duke, came to visit me. She was a great violinist, the only real artist in our family. Growing up in Nashville, we had been close friends. Before I was drafted, Matilda married and asked me to help decorate her new home. I had her dining room painted Schiaparelli pink. This was my first real decorating job.

On her visit to Outwood, Matilda said that she had recently become a Christian Scientist. She told me a lot about her new church and its founder, Mary Baker Eddy. All of this was quite revealing since we had both grown up in the Presbyterian church. I shared with her that while I was in England I had attended the Roman Catholic church with a man in my battalion, and that here in Kentucky I occasionally attended the Roman Catholic church with a fellow patient in the hospital. I admitted that I did not like the ritual or ceremonial part of the services. Knowing that I was searching for something, when Matilda returned home she sent me a copy of In His Name *by Lillian DeWaters. The book completely changed my life. Reading it, I was electrified by what I discovered: truth. The book gave me courage to believe in myself and see things in a strong positive light.*

In the early spring of 1945, without an official discharge from the hospital, I moved into the New Century Hotel in the nearby village of Dawson Springs. Mother and Betsy came and helped me get settled in my new surroundings. As an outpatient, I reported to the hospital for regular checkups and physical examinations. My condition improved rapidly and by the next spring I left Dawson Springs and returned to Nashville.

The doctors warned me over and over that my lung condition would prevent me from ever flying in an airplane.

World War II ended in 1945. A year later, in May 1946, Hadley returned to Nashville, moved into his parents' house, and got back his old job selling furniture at Bradfords. In August of that year, Harold Caulfield, a friend from Nashville who was an architect in New York City, wrote and asked Hadley to join him on a vacation in Bridgeton, Maine.

I went to Maine for one reason: I knew I had to go through New York City to get there. Traveling by train from Nashville, I shall never forget seeing the skyline as we approached the city. Harold met me at Pennsylvania Station, and we then took a train from Grand Central Terminal to Boston. When we got there, before taking the bus on to Bridgeton, we went to the new Bonwit Teller store that had just been decorated by William Pahlmann. I had yet to meet the man, but I was thrilled to see his work—to actually stand in a space he had designed. In early September we returned to New York. I decided to stay in the city for a few weeks before returning to Nashville. I checked into the West Sixty-third Street YMCA where I lived until the middle of November. This was one of the happiest times of my life.

"Sunny Gables," Hadley house, Nashville, Tennessee

There can be little doubt that Hadley was filled with a vibrant anticipation. He was in the city of his dreams. He was on the threshold of meeting many of the decorators he had so long admired but only read about in magazines. As he talked about his encounters with these established New Yorkers, the charming naïveté that he exhibited at this moment is equaled only by the inner courage that led him to knock, unannounced, on the doors of his future.

William Pahlmann at Lord & Taylor

I made it my business during those two months to meet every decorator I had ever read about. I started at Lord & Taylor, where I hoped to meet William Pahlmann. I was told that he was no longer with the store, and they had no information on him. Remembering that a native of Tennessee, Frances Hurd, an editor at House Beautiful, *had published much of Pahlmann's work, and that they were personal friends, I called her office. My only credential for an appointment was that I was from Nashville. Miss Hurd agreed to see me and told me that Pahlmann had opened his own firm on Third Avenue between Fifty-eighth and Fifty-ninth streets. At last I met Bill Pahlmann. He proved to be a man of great charm with a flamboyant personality and certainly he was not shy about anything. He was enthusiastic when I told him I wanted to be an interior decorator and recommended that I consider his alma mater, Parsons School of Design. He encouraged me to come and see him again when I returned to New York City.*

Without an appointment, I went to Ruby Ross Wood's office. Luckily Billy Baldwin was in and agreed to see me. The offices were painted a pale blue with ivory trim and there were masses of fresh flowers everywhere. Billy was about my height and build but slightly smaller. I remember that he was immaculately dressed. Like Pahlmann, he could not have been more encouraging and insisted that if I did return to New York, I would call for an appointment and see him again. I did and was finally able to meet the fascinating Mrs. Wood.

My meeting with Mrs. Eleanor Brown at McMillen, arranged by

George Stacey, whom I had met on the recommendation of Billy Baldwin, was the most focused of my encounters. At the time McMillen was the foremost decorating firm in the country. I was fortunate that Mrs. Brown agreed to meet with me. When I told her I wanted to be an interior decorator, she listened attentively and said her only advice was to go to Parsons School of Design. She had graduated from Parsons, was on the board of Parsons, lectured at Parsons, and only hired decorators who graduated from the school. She wished me well but there was little time for small talk. With the lion's share of the decorating contracts and the most prestigious client list in the country, McMillen, Inc. was overwhelmed with work after the war. Eleanor Brown was a very busy lady.

The most unusual of the decorators that I met was Rose Cumming. She had to be one of the most eccentric and talented decorators in the world. In addition to the wares in her shop—antiques, fabrics, accessories, and furniture—she also sold flowers. She had rigged a faux waterfall that fell from an enormous plate glass window that was the background for her floral display. There was no air conditioning in those days—the door of her shop was open to the street and inside she had a great many oscillating electric fans. The breeze from the fans made the crystal prisms on the several hanging chandeliers tinkle which gave the shop an exotic air.

Billy Baldwin in his apartment, Amster Yard

When I entered, Miss Cumming was sitting in a chair at her desk, a beautiful Louis XV bureau plat. On the desk, next to a large vase of lilies, were Miss Cumming's tinsel slippers. I offered a brief personal introduction. Her response was, "Feel free to look around." Her enormous mop of hair was dyed light purple-blue and her outfit—a loose, low cut dress of sorts—looked more like curtain fabric than dress material. Everything in the shop was beautiful and over the top. Years later when I came to know, admire, and respect her more and more, I also came to know that she did indeed drape herself in swaths of curtain or upholstery fabric, held by pins where necessary, secured with silk cords and tassels.

Rose Cumming taught everyone in the decorating

trade more about eclecticism than any other designer. She was a genius when it came to mixing colors, textures, and periods. She could put the most priceless antique next to the most commonplace accessory, and it was a marriage made in heaven. When I left she was still sitting at her desk, eyeing me, and said, "I'll see you when you get back to New York." Her departing words I took as a resolute affirmation.

In addition to meeting decorators that I had long dreamed of encountering and going to antiques shops, I spent hours in the Metropolitan Museum of Art, the Frick Collection, and the Museum of Modern Art. I did a lot of walking—I couldn't get enough of New York City. For me, the city was dazzling.

On an afternoon at the Metropolitan Museum I met James Rogers Lamantia, another Southerner who, like me, was seeing New York for the first time. Having just graduated from the School of Architecture at Tulane University in New Orleans in June, Jimmy was working for a firm in the city. During my eight weeks in New York, he and I spent many Saturdays and Sundays walking, looking at buildings, and talking about architectural design. Jimmy had a great gift for teaching, and I can honestly say that he taught me to see in a new way. I distinctly remember that he encouraged me to look for the intricacy and subtlety of design everywhere—in the most unexpected places, like manhole covers, for instance. In New York City there are thousands of different manhole covers with different design patterns. Jimmy talked a lot about surface ornamentation versus structural design, what makes a building well designed, and how our understanding of space is influenced by natural light and shadow.

Hadley, like so many people, had come to New York City with an agenda, but his inherent curiosity and insatiable desire to learn led him to keep his options open. A chance encounter opened his eyes to new ways of perceiving images and space. Trust in the vision that he acquired led to a new concept of living, of being Albert Hadley.

Jimmy also introduced me to Brooks Brothers. At that time, one of my favorite outfits was a camel-hair sports coat that I wore with a white shirt and a tie with black-and-white zebras printed on a bright red background. I thought it was pretty nifty but my friend obviously thought differently. Without making me feel foolish, in a very gentle manner, he let me know that I needed to give some thought to my wardrobe and pointed the way to Brooks Brothers. He specifically mentioned their black knit ties. The experience would forever change the way I dressed and thought about what I wore. When I returned to New York to go to Parsons, Jimmy was still working in the city. In 1948 he was elected a Fellow at the American Academy in Rome. After a year there, he returned to Tulane where he joined the faculty in the School of Architecture.

During the second week in November, Harold Caulfield, the friend who invited me to Maine, called to say that he was flying to Nashville for his wedding. I had accepted his invitation to be one of the ushers in the wedding and he suggested that we fly together. Ignoring the army doctor's orders, I thought, if I am going to die, and I knew that one day I would, why not die on an airplane. On the way to the airport, we passed a large cemetery, which I took as a bad omen. Taking off in the plane, seeing New York below, flying to Nashville, and arriving home in what I thought was the ultimate chic in travel was an enormous thrill. Fantastic!

I should have listened to the doctors. By the time we arrived in Nashville, due to inadequate air pressure in the passenger cabin, I was quite ill. My lung infection had come back. For several weeks I was in bed, which meant missing Harold's wedding. Tuberculosis was a major health concern in those days. Our family doctor arranged with a couple, friends of his, for me to have a room in their house in Delray Beach, Florida. Early in January 1947, I left for Florida. Knowing no one in Delray Beach,

Rose Cumming in her shop

and hardly knowing my host and hostess, I occasionally went to the bowling alley as a spectator. One afternoon when I was there I encountered Clifton Webb and Bea Lillie. At the time Bea Lillie, with her fabulous wit and style, was the toast of the West End in London and adored on Broadway in New York. Always on stage, at the bowling alley Bea Lillie held everyone's attention. I am sure I was not alone in my surprise of seeing these two stars of stage and screen in a bowling alley.

While most of my days were spent in total leisure, sketching and drawing on the beach, I did write to Parsons School of Design for a catalog. Since I first read Van Day Truex's article "Mirrors of Personality" in the magazine Interiors, in 1942, I had always wanted to go to Parsons. In the article, Van wrote about the apartments of Elsie de Wolfe, Elsa Schiaparelli, and Diana Vreeland, and his own philosophy of design. A short time after returning the application for admissions, I received notice that I was accepted into the summer program that began in June. Returning to Nashville in early April, I used the remaining months of spring to prepare for my June departure, or rather my June arrival. With the aid of the GI Bill I was headed for New York City.

The Capital of the World

In 1947 the major cities of Europe were recovering from the most destructive war in history. Much of London and Berlin laid in rubble. Cologne, Dresden, Rotterdam, and Warsaw were in ruins; Rome and Paris were cities in disgrace. The majority of the world population gave credit to the United States for the defeat of the Axis powers and the end of World War II. Many of those same people had little knowledge of Americans and the complex makeup of the United States, but they all knew New York. Crowned with the laurels of victory, basking in an allure like no place else on earth, New York City was the capital of the world. That June, realizing a long delayed dream, Hadley arrived in New York. His destination was 136 East Fifty-seventh Street, the home of Parsons School of Design. He was twenty-seven years old.

The great influx of male students, men returning from the war with the benefits of the GI Bill, had forced Parsons to seek auxiliary classroom space. First-year classes were held across the East River in a warehouse in Long Island City. After arranging for a room at the YMCA on West Sixty-third Street, Hadley made his way to the school. It wasn't until one of the first sessions for new students in September that Van Day Truex, the president of the school, met the students. Hadley remembers it vividly.

I can see him now. Van Day Truex was a very handsome man—tall with chiseled features. It was a hot day and there was no air-conditioning. He was wearing an impeccably tailored brown Italian tweed suit. One of his jacket sleeves was unbuttoned and rolled back to reveal the white cuff of his shirt and a cuff link made of an antique Roman coin set in gold mounts. I would later learn that he referred to cuff links as "cuff buttons." The colors and textures of his suit, shirt, tie, and socks were exquisitely coordinated, and his shoes were made of the finest Italian leather. As I sat listening to his well-chosen words, it was impossible for me to imagine that one day I would know Van Truex on a first-name basis, be a member of his faculty at Parsons, have the benefit of his opinions and wisdom as a colleague in interior design, and enjoy the privilege of his friendship. That day, my focus was not on the future but the present. I was there to listen, to try to understand everything that I was told, and to learn everything I could about interior design. That was my sole reason for being in New York City.

After the summer session and a brief break, the new semester began in early September. There were about sixty people in my class. Most of our

Van Day Truex

work was done on drawing tables in large rooms where we were supervised and closely monitored. Our assignments were carefully and thoughtfully critiqued. Everyone in the class worked on the same project, which allowed us to compare our solutions. Once, when we were designing the interior for a ladies' fashion boutique, I decided to give mine an Oriental look. Van, who was regularly in and out of the classrooms and always present for final critiques, came by my desk while I was working and said, "Be careful, don't end up looking like an upper Broadway chop suey house." It was this kind of precise observation from Van and other members of the faculty that made me want to work even harder.

There can be no question that when Hadley entered Parsons it was the premier school of interior design and fashion design in America. No other school came close to Parsons's prestigious position. The faculty and the programs they offered were simply the best in the country and everybody at Parsons knew it. To be there was a heady experience.

The history of interior design, emphasizing Italian, French, and English architecture and furnishings, was the absolute foundation of our studies. The faculty was relentless in its demand that we be able to identify periods of design and articulate an understanding of the context in which these designs originated. A vocabulary of the correct names for architectural elements and interior details was required. Life drawing, architectural drawing, and perspective interior rendering were a part of the core curriculum. The class frequently went on guided tours to the Metropolitan Museum of Art, the Frick Collection, and the Museum of Natural History. In addition to the lectures, we were encouraged to spend hours sketching in the museums. On occasion the class was divided into small groups, and accompanied by an instructor, we visited the private homes and apartments of people who had great style, taste, and wonderful collections of art and antiques.

In order to finish the three-year course as quickly as possible, I continued in summer school after my first academic year. I also moved from

PRECEDING PAGES
Hadley student project,
"Contemporary Penthouse"

LEFT
Hadley design for the office
of a woman executive

FOLLOWING PAGES
Hadley student project,
"The Empire Period"

the YMCA to a brownstone boarding house at 305 East Fifty-first Street,
owned by Harold Caufield, my old friend from Nashville.

When I graduated in June 1949, I was given the Elsie de Wolfe prize
to study for a summer at the branch of Parsons in Paris. The award
included travel in France, England, and Italy. Unfortunately, it did not
cover all of the expenses, and I was unable to accept. I needed to go to
work and earn some money.

Hadley's first job was working as an assistant at Roslyn Rosier's shop,
Town and Country, on Third Avenue and Fiftieth Street. Like Rose
Cumming and William Pahlmann, Roslyn Rosier had amazing, eclectic
taste. She could put the most unusual pieces together and make a room
work. Hadley could not have had a better beginning job. Mrs. Rosier
instilled in him the truth that things don't need to be expensive to have
great flair. This is not to say that Mrs. Rosier didn't like expensive
things—she did and had some very fine things in her shop. Her gift was
mixing expensive pieces with things that had very little value—the effect
was always terrific.

On weekends, Mrs. Rosier closed her shop and went shopping in the
country. She always came back with the most fantastic things. In addi-
tion to her eye for buying, she knew how to display the merchandise in
her shop. Her knack for draping fabrics, placing furniture, and creating
tabletop displays was magical. Once she filled the window of her shop
with white sand and placed an eighteenth century Italian armchair that
was set askew so that it appeared to be toppling over. She dotted the sand
with objects of rare allure. It was like surreal art—pure fantasy.

I had been with Mrs. Rosier three months when Van Truex called and
asked me to join the interior design faculty at Parsons. I remember
telling Mrs. Rosier while we were in her car. She was driving.
Immediately she stopped the car saying that I could have caused her to
have a wreck with such news. During the remaining days that I worked
for her, she tried to convince me to decline the teaching position, but I
had made up my mind. I knew that a faculty position at Parsons, and the
opportunity to have extended exposure to the Parsons philosophy of
design, could only benefit my future. In early September 1949 I reported
to Harold Guy, the director of the department of interior design, and
began my new job at Parsons School of Design.

Pieces of the Puzzle

PRECEDING PAGES
Tree of Life

During his first year on the faculty at Parsons, 1949 to 1950, Hadley celebrated his thirtieth birthday. Since coming to New York, his sense of privacy, shunning social commitments, and avoiding the complications of relationships had not changed. One of Hadley's few friends was Billy Baldwin, who had been a frequent guest lecturer at Parsons when Hadley was a student. Now Baldwin and Hadley met as colleagues when Baldwin came to lecture. Having heard Truex's accolades about Hadley's student work and observing his teaching skills and tasteful eye, Baldwin had a growing respect for the young man's abilities and talents.

With the financial security of a teaching position, Hadley rented an apartment above a grocery store on University Place between Tenth and Eleventh Streets. Having a living room, bedroom, small kitchen, and full bath added to the bliss of being in Greenwich Village. It was time for him to flex his decorating muscle and show his colors.

The living room had long casement windows and a working fireplace. I used a tall folding screen to close off the kitchen. Each panel of the screen was a different color. At Lord & Taylor, for sixty-five dollars each, I bought a pair of antique black Regency chairs with cane seats. My other purchase was a pair of tufted chairs that were upholstered in black horsehair. I painted all of the rooms white—white walls, white trim, white ceiling—quite surprising in those days. In contrast, Billy Baldwin had just painted his living room at Amster Yard gardenia-leaf green. Photographs of the room and Billy's comments about how important it was to use bold colors had been in several magazines. When Billy saw my white walls, his only comment was "Interesting."

Soon after his first visit to my apartment, Billy called and said he wanted to give me something but hesitated because he did not wish to offend me. He went on to say that someone had given him an antique Louis XV bureau plat and he wanted to know if I wanted his Directoire writing table. Of course I was not offended; I was delighted. Billy's gift was my first piece of really nice furniture and the beginning of something that has been going on in my life ever since—passing things along to people who need them or want them. Over the years I have given away and swapped innumerable things with friends. I have not been alone in this. I remember Van trading his Knole–style sofa for Billy's four antique Louis XVI chairs that had belonged to William Odom.

Peter Ball and an assistant
at "Hospital Flowers"

The tufted chairs that I bought for my first apartment, over fifty years ago, have taken on a life of their own. Over the years I sent them out several times to be re-covered and on occasion had them copied for clients. Once when I was in the upholsterer's workroom, he referred to a pair of these chairs as "Hadley" chairs. The name stuck. I still have them made for clients and the name remains, the "Hadley" chair.

Even though Hadley had a full-time teaching job, his salary was small and there certainly were no benefits. The great advantage that young people like Hadley had in starting out in New York at that time was that the city was not the expensive place to live that it has become. A good theater ticket could be had for less than five dollars, standing room cost almost nothing, and most museums were free. A three-course meal at Schraft's was about three dollars, including tip, and if this was too much, a person could eat at the Automat for less than a dollar. Even at those prices, which today seem inconceivably low, Hadley and others like him who came to New York to make it big, had a struggle. While it was never easy financially, it was a time filled with opportunity. In the post-war years, if a young person had talent, New York was the only place to be.

In those days, a beginning teacher did not make a large salary. To supplement my income, I took on extra work—moonlighting—if it did not conflict with my Parsons schedule. One of my jobs came through Lester Grundy, who was the senior decorator at Dorothy Draper and a frequent lecturer at Parsons. He invited me to join him and one of his college

classmates, Peter Ball, at the Williams Club for lunch. Peter had come up with the idea of putting refrigerated glass display cases for miniature flower arrangements in the lobbies of hospitals. His plan was for people to buy the arrangements for patients they were visiting. Lester had designed display cases for the flowers that looked like Louis XV armoires. I was hired to be the floral designer. On the appointed days I went to Peter's workrooms and made the prototype flower arrangement that was duplicated by a crew of women workers. Under Peter's direction, the finished arrangements were delivered to hospitals all over the city. Many years later, Peter Ball came into my life again. When my house in Southport, Connecticut, was featured in a magazine I received a call from a lady who said she recognized the letter basket on the front door. She said she had put it there when she and her husband owned the house. It is true that the letter basket was there when I bought the house and I never saw any reason to change it. The lady who called was Mrs. Peter Ball.

Because he was born soon after the First World War, into a society struggling to overcome tragic loss, Hadley learned at an early age that regardless of any circumstances, a person must have the conviction to succeed, to get a job done and done well. If Hadley accepts a job he will find a way to accomplish the task. This unrelenting work ethic is supported by his refusal to allow distractions to interfere with his work.

After my first year of teaching at Parsons I was invited to go, as a faculty advisor, on the school's annual summer study tour of France and Italy. Betty Carter, a senior member of the faculty, was in charge of the trip and I was to be the junior assistant. In those days, no matter how hot it was, gentlemen always wore a jacket and tie. Most of my clothes were casual and I certainly didn't have a wardrobe of suitable outfits for six weeks in Europe. Billy came to my rescue and let me borrow one of his navy blue summer suits. When I arrived in Paris, Van was waiting for me at the hotel. He came up to my room and watched as I unpacked and hung up my clothes. As I put Billy's suit on a hanger, Van said, "I am glad you brought a nice outfit. It reminds me of Billy." I didn't confess where the suit came from but Van knew.

Immediately after we arrived in Paris, Betty Carter's senior assistant quit. I was told that I would take his place, which meant being the guide and lecturer on all field trips. Having never been to France and Italy, I was petrified. The night before each trip I would go over the list of buildings, interiors, and significant furniture, sculpture, and art that we were to see the following day. Often I read late into the night so that I would be prepared. When we arrived at the village or chateau and the students were out of the bus, I would instruct them to take some free time before the guided tour began. I would then make a mad dash to familiarize myself with whatever it was that we were there to see. When the students gathered, my lecture had such authority that they thought I had been to the place many times.

PRECEDING PAGES
Hadley's East Seventy-first Street apartment

New York was in great flux in the post-war years and new buildings were going up all over town. Lever House, the Seagram Building, the Chase Bank on Fifth Avenue at Forty-third Street, the Guggenheim Museum, and the United Nations headquarters were all built in that period. Soon after Philip Johnson's Glass House in New Canaan, Connecticut, was finished in 1949, a group from Parsons was invited for a private tour. While Hadley had long admired the work that came out of the De Stijl movement, the Wiener Werkstätte and the Bauhaus, his intimate exposure to the Glass House sealed his commitment to the new international style of architecture.

In 1953 there were strange political rumblings at Parsons and the following year Van left the school. The chance to work with Van was the main reason I had accepted the job at Parsons. After his untimely departure, I was uncomfortable with things that were happening in the administration of the school. At the beginning of the 1954 spring semester I resigned. In June, when my teaching came to an end, I was on my own and needed to get a job or open my own decorating business. The time had come to leave my Village digs and move uptown. Other than a few antiques shops in the University Place area, the interior design resources were all in midtown, on Fifty-seventh Street or Madison Avenue.

Cultivating friendships has always been one of Hadley's skills. In no way can his gift for the nurturing of relationships pass for what is known today as networking. Scheming for personal gain and political or social connections would be foreign to Hadley. His attraction to people is, more frequently than not, instigated by a mutual interest or a serendipitous encounter that evolves into a lasting bond. Along with this character trait, Hadley has a remarkable sense of timing and judgment. All of these—sincere relationships, time, and judgment—coupled with his insistence on manners and the dictum of Elsie de Wolfe, "suitability," have opened many doors for him.

A woman whom I greatly admired, known as Madame Avakoff, had a small antiques shop on the ground floor, below the street level, in an old brownstone on East Fifty-seventh Street. Madame Avakoff's shop, Vieux Paris, was a treasure trove of eighteenth-century French furniture and objects. In those days she was one of the few dealers in New York who offered antiques of such quality and rare beauty—not too expensive or grand, but extraordinary.

When Madame Avakoff learned of my impending move, she arranged for me to have a small studio apartment in the rear of the second floor of the building. The apartment was directly above a dry cleaning establishment that occupied the rear section of the first floor. That was no problem for me; after all, I had lived quite happily above a food market on University Place.

Unfortunately, many New Yorkers only enjoy the things that are obvious in their great city. They wait for the critics to say it is all right to see a performance, a movie, or eat in a restaurant. For Hadley, the unknown, the new, the different, and the unusual all hold mystery and excitement. This was true when he first came to New York and has not changed in fifty years. In the unexpected thing, or place, or person he often finds his greatest inspiration.

Just before I moved into my Fifty-seventh Street apartment, the Kabuki players were making their first appearance in New York since World War II. I was fortunate to see an early performance. What a thrill it was to watch the precise, exquisite Japanese manner and movement and to see the brilliant staging. The entire production was intensified by the use of color. Everything was color. Color expressed through harmony, through contrast, through light and seemingly through sound and motion. Visually there was every imaginable hue and shade—a rainbow of colors offered as a priceless gift. Brilliant flashes of black and white added wit and spark to the Kabuki colossal color extravaganza.

My new apartment was to be multifunctional. Within a short time, it would also serve as my first office. The small entrance hall was little more than a hyphen while the main room was of good, generous proportions. It lacked any significant features except for three rather beautiful, tall windows on the long wall opposite the entrance. There was good north light and reflected sunlight from the garden facades of the houses that faced Fifty-eighth Street. This light was dappled from spring through early autumn as it played through the branches of a grove of trees.

Inspired by the Kabuki players, whitewashed walls and dark polished floors became the background for my new decorating scheme. Centered on the end wall, to the left as one entered the room, was a large, low, rather square profile sofa that was slipcovered in a rich, deep blue felt. A large pair of pillows covered in a black-and-white printed cotton, of Japanese design, highlighted the blue mass. On the wall above the sofa was a large Portuguese mirror. The frame of the mirror was made of ebony that had been inlaid with mother-of-pearl. Covering the floor in front of the sofa was a newly acquired rectangular rug made of black and white monkey skins. My chairs were covered in black horsehair and a few small tables completed this group.

On the wall at the opposite end of the room, facing the sofa, was a handsome nineteenth-century American wardrobe made of beautiful dark wood. To the left of this, set at an angle across the corner of the room and pulled forward to embrace the nearby window, was the writing table that Billy Baldwin had given me and one of my black-and-white Regency chairs. Behind the table was a low four-panel screen. The panels were painted a high-gloss light fern green. A lamp, properly placed, was on the left side of the table. On the right side was a tall bottle-shaped, bright blue Chinese porcelain vase that I had chosen mainly for color impact. In the vase were a few loosely arranged tall branches from flowering trees or shrubs. Centered on the tabletop, on a Lucite easel, was the only note of scarlet in the room—a small watercolor

rendering of a nineteenth-century interior. My assembled possessions fur-
nished the room with a sense of comfort and ease, but something was
missing. It was those Kabuki players stirring up trouble!

From a theatrical supply company, I bought yards and yards of gos-
samer-thin China silk, the color of petunias—Schiaparelli pink, to be
exact—that I used for unlined curtains. The curtains hung from simple
poles at the top of the windows and billowed down to the polished floor.
I thought the effect was sensational. There was no other pink in the
room—just the rich jewel-like colors, plus black and white.

I actually got a bit of Kabuki movement. It turned out that during
the day and often at night, my three beautiful, antique windows were not
without their flaw. The apparatuses used in the dry cleaning establish-
ment below my apartment caused the pink Kabuki curtains to dance and
flutter on the floor. Their movement was beautiful—a strange tempo, a
wicked beat. Kabuki all the way!

I settled myself into my new Kabuki setting and for a few months I
went back to work for Roslyn Rosier. She had moved her shop to Fifty-
seventh Street, between Park and Lexington Avenues. While I was
devoted to Mrs. Rosier, I knew that her real interest was retail—buying
for her shop and selling. This was everything to her. What I really wanted
to do was be a decorator. In 1955 I took the plunge and opened Albert
Hadley, Inc.

During the years that Hadley taught at Parsons, he got to know Mrs.
Brown at McMillen. She was on the board of directors at the school and a
frequent guest lecturer and critic. She and Hadley often spoke of his "just
turning up at her office" to get advice on how to be a decorator. Knowing
the great respect that Truex had for Hadley, and having seen the outstanding teaching job he had done, Mrs. Brown made it her business to
find out where he had gone after he resigned from the faculty.

Without a client list, getting work was not easy and I struggled to make
ends meet. It was a lucky break for me in 1956 when Mrs. Brown called
from McMillen and asked me to come for an interview. I got the job!

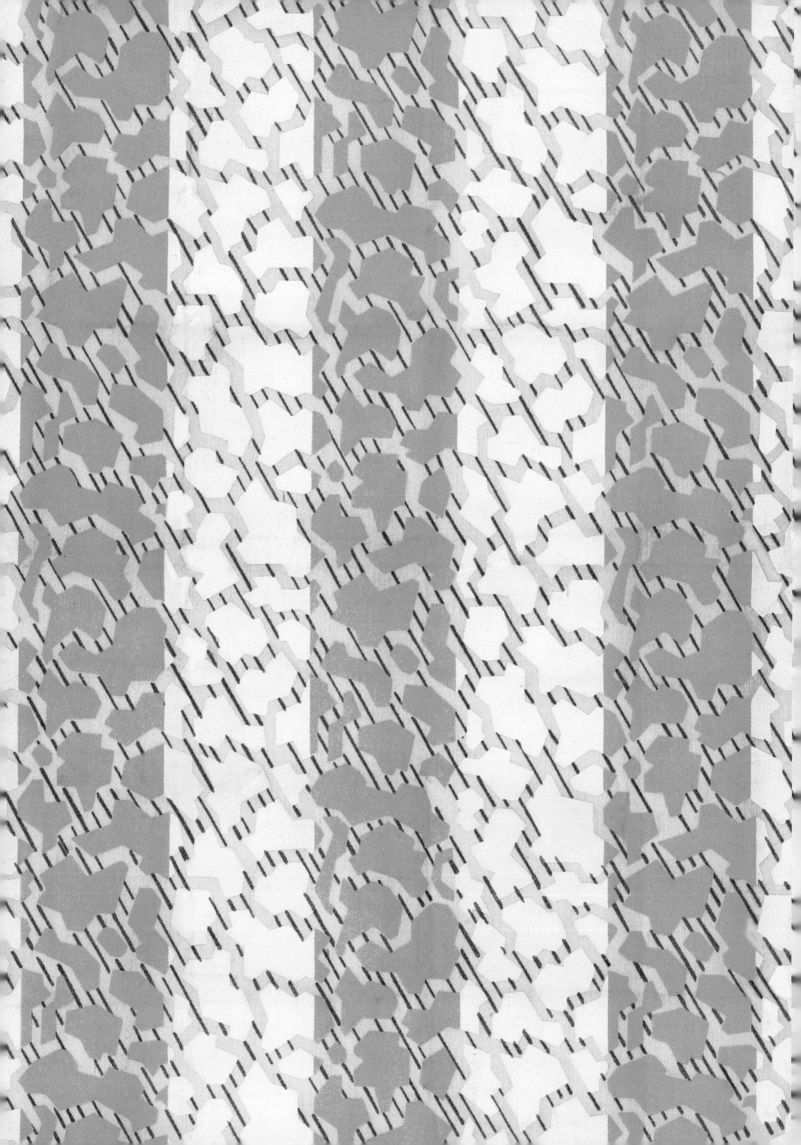

Moving Up and Out

In 1956, the same year that Hadley began working for Mrs. Brown, his friend Wilbur Pippin asked him to share a duplex apartment on East Fifty-eighth Street. The apartment provided more space than either of the men could afford on their individual salaries and had the added bonus of a garden. Joining Mrs. Brown's staff and sharing the new apartment were both propitious moves.

When Hadley went to work for Mrs. Brown, McMillen, Inc. was unquestionably the most prestigious decorating firm in America, with a long history. In 1914 Eleanor Brown, the daughter of a wealthy family in St. Louis, Missouri, married Drury McMillen, an architect who was also from St. Louis. Even though McMillen's work took them to Brazil, the young couple bought a brownstone in New York City. With their son, Louis, who was born in 1916, the McMillens frequently returned to the city between assignments. It was during one of these trips that Eleanor discovered the New York School of Fine and Applied Arts, now Parsons School of Design. She always said she registered at the school not really knowing what she was doing and took the courses piecemeal. After completing the three-year course in New York, Eleanor went to study under William Odom at the Paris branch of the school in the Place des Vosges. After graduating she returned to Rio de Janeiro where the American ambassador asked her to decorate the embassy. This was her first professional work. In 1924 Eleanor and her son returned to New York City, where she worked as an assistant to Elsie Cobb Wilson. She had not been there long when William Odom urged her to open her own business. She asked her father to lend her the finances required to open her decorating firm. He agreed to her request on the condition that she take a yearlong business course at Katherine Gibbs Secretarial School for Women. Immediately after finishing the business course, she opened McMillen, Inc. In 1928 her marriage to Drury McMillen ended in divorce. In 1934 she married the architect Archibald Manning Brown. The Parsons School of Design was always of paramount interest to Mrs. Brown. She took her responsibilities as chairman of the board very seriously. She was devoted to Van Day Truex and deeply regretted his leaving the school. When she heard that Hadley had also resigned, she was prompted to immediately call and see if he would join her staff.

When Mrs. Brown called me to come for an interview at McMillen, she said I would assist Grace Fakes, who directed the firm's design department. Like

Mrs. Archibald Brown

Mrs. Brown, Grace Fakes was a graduate of the New York School of Fine and Applied Arts. Before joining McMillen, she taught interior design at the school. Miss Fakes, as she was called, knew everything there was to know about period furniture and the history of interior design. She absolutely ruled the design department at McMillen, where she created incredible custom moldings, paneling, and lighting fixtures. Her only fault, if it could be viewed as a fault, was her inability to get along with clients. She simply could not deal with people. On the day I reported for work, Mrs. Brown told me that I was to be Ethel Smith's assistant. Ethel was the senior decorator at McMillen and Mrs. Brown's right-hand person. If I wasn't going to work with Miss Fakes, I could not have had a better assignment than assisting Ethel Smith. She had a great eye and a fantastic sense of direction.

In the decorating trade, the work of overseeing painting and wallpapering, hanging curtains, and placing lighting fixtures, rugs, and furniture is referred to as "the installation of the project." Often a trusted and experienced assistant, in close contact with the senior decorator, is the project manager. This is no small responsibility. Because he or she is on the job site with the workmen and craftsmen, and frequently the client, who is there to "see how things are going," the project manager must have the manners and finesse of a diplomat and the drive of Attila the Hun to see that everything is done on time. Hadley's first assignment was to work as the project manager on one of Ethel Smith's decorating contracts.

Douglas Dillon, the ambassador to France and later secretary of the treasury, and his wife, Phyllis, had recently bought a house in Hobe Sound, Florida. They commissioned McMillen to do the interior design. Mrs. Brown assigned Ethel Smith to be the decorator on the Dillon project. With a husband and family in Connecticut, it was difficult for Ethel to make frequent trips to Hobe Sound. As her assistant, I became the project manager and did the necessary traveling. Before I arrived at McMillen, Ethel had done all of the room schemes and selected the fabrics, furniture, and accessories. Seeing that everything was installed according to her specifications was my job. I remember that the overall effect of the Dillon house was bright, crisp, and very up-to-date. When the work in Hobe Sound was finished, I continued working with Ethel on a project that she was doing for Mr. and Mrs. Milton Underwood.

One of the unfortunate aspects of interior design is the sense of impermanence that is inherent in the trade. No matter how beautifully a house may be decorated, eventually all property changes hands and the new owner wants a different look. While these constant changes are the lifeblood that provides the cash flow of the decorating trade, very few interior designs have long lives. But Hadley's next job would prove to have lasting significance.

Extremely wealthy Texans, the Underwoods had recently purchased Rosedown Plantation in St. Francisville, Louisiana. Mrs. Underwood had been in Natchez [Mississippi] with her garden club when quite by chance she saw Rosedown. Peering through the locked gates, she could see that the house and the gardens were in serious neglect. An enthusiastic amateur horticulturist, Catherine Underwood envisioned the gardens restored to their original state. After hearing the history of the plantation and stories of the gardens when they were under the care of Martha Turnbull, wife of the original owner, Daniel Turnbull, Catherine fell in love with the place. She telephoned her husband and said she had seen a plantation that she wanted to buy. His response was, "Then you should

Hadley during his years at Parsons

buy it." The following day she did. This was the first time that anyone other than descendants of Daniel and Martha Turnbull had owned the plantation house since it was built in 1836.

Knowing that the restoration of the house and gardens would take years, Mr. and Mrs. Underwood built a new house on the property to live in while the work was in progress. McMillen was hired to decorate the new house. Again, Ethel was the decorator and I was the project manager. Each time I went to St. Francisville, which was often, I always stayed with the Underwoods. They were absolutely charming people and in no time at all the three of us became good friends.

One morning at breakfast Mrs. Underwood asked me if I would like to see the big house, Rosedown Plantation. Being a Southerner and loving the antebellum architecture of the Old South, I was thrilled. The two of us made our way through the overgrown hedgerows and gardens to a clearing where I got my first view of Rosedown. It was fantastic. Built in the style of a Carolina Tidewater house, it had a neoclassical columned facade and double front galleries. The long unpaved entrance road was lined on both sides by gracefully arching, ancient oak trees that formed a grand colonnade. Between the trees there were larger than life-size Italian marble statues that Martha and Daniel Turnbull had brought back from Europe in 1830. On that same trip, their honeymoon, the Turnbulls stopped in New York City where they saw the play Rosedown.

Miss Grace Fakes

Decorators are frequently criticized for wanting to get rid of everything a client owns and start afresh, everything new. The decorator's obvious advantage is to make more money. A truly fine decorator would never approach a job from this perspective. All clients have a history and their possessions are a part of that history. Unless the client's aim is to get rid of everything and start over, as can be the case, then the decorator must approach their furnishings and accessories with respect. Having grown up in the Great Depression, Hadley is and always has been acutely aware of the things people have and the emotional attachment they may have to them. His extreme care in these matters is evident in his sensitive advice to Mr. and Mrs. Underwood.

As Mrs. Underwood and I toured the house, I was enchanted. The punkah, still hanging over the dining-room table, faintly showed some of the original design, which was a painting of an eagle. We would later learn that John James Audubon had tutored the Turnbulls' two daughters and well may have painted the eagle. The attic, a veritable treasure trove,

Ethel Smith with her family

was filled with trunks and crates of furnishings, clothing, toys, and dolls. In the kitchen cabinets were the old pots and pans that had been used by generations of Turnbulls. Most of the wallpaper was peeling, which allowed us to see remnants of earlier papers. That night over dinner, I suggested to the Underwoods that they build a series of buildings, like Quonset huts, for the contents of the house to be stored in while the restoration was being done. The one thing I urged, above all else, was to not throw away anything.

With the Underwoods' permission, I began spending a part of each day in the house. I made sketches of every room and took extensive notes on the architectural details. Mr. and Mrs. Underwood liked my proposals for the decor but were adamant that restoration, not renovation, be applied to all of the work done on the house and the gardens. In addition to Ethel and me, a team of architects, engineers, and expert gardeners were hired for the project. Enormous greenhouses were built for plant storage while the gardens were in transition. If the plant materials listed in Martha Turnbull's extensive inventory of the original gardens were not available, the Underwoods had them propagated in the greenhouses.

One of my responsibilities was gathering as much information as I could on the original plans and construction of the house. Records revealed that timber cut on the plantation had been shipped upriver to Cincinnati, Ohio, to be made into doors, moldings, and trim. The finished products were then shipped back down the Mississippi to Rosedown. The fireplace marble and the mahogany for the main staircase came from cities in the Northeast or from overseas. After the house was finished in 1836, it was furnished with the finest things available. Many of the pieces came from famous cabinetmakers like Crawford Riddle and Anthony Quervelle of Philadelphia and Prudent Mallard of New Orleans. Fortunately, most of the original furniture was still in the house.

In addition to my many trips to St. Francisville, Mrs. Underwood made frequent shopping visits to New York. At the same time we were working on Rosedown, Mrs. Lila Acheson Wallace and her team of decorators and designers were restoring a nineteenth-century house, Boscobel, on the Hudson River. In many ways Boscobel and Rosedown were competing for the same antique furnishings, fabrics, and wall coverings. It was not uncommon to find the perfect piece of furniture or decorative accessory in an antiques shop only to be told that it was already sold to Mrs. Wallace.

One of the great finds that Mrs. Smith and I made in a New York City antiques shop was an early-nineteenth-century carved wooden figure of a bird, like a stork, that was a child's crib. The body of the bird was shaped to hold a baby. On the day the crib arrived at Rosedown, I told one of Mrs. Underwood's assistants that the bed had been given to the Turnbulls by John James Audubon. I went on to add that Audubon had the crib custommade to celebrate the arrival of the couple's firstborn child. The whole story was made up—not a word of truth. Years later when I took my mother and sister to see Rosedown, our tour guide pointed to the crib and with great authority repeated my far-fetched yarn about Audubon.

Everything that we put into the house was of the period. Nancy McClelland, who was the leading authority on antique wallpapers, was able to find the same scenic paper that had been originally used in the

Rosedown Plantation

Hadley sketch for Rosedown parlor
and photo of the finished room

entrance hall. Eleanor Merrill, who had an antiques shop on Fifty-seventh Street and was an expert on old textiles, supplied us with most of the fabrics. Throughout the project I worked closely with the architects, engineers, and builders to be sure that no modern devices were evident. No light switches, no electrical outlets, and no wires or cords were to be seen.

Even with meticulous planning, and certainly this went into the restoration of Rosedown Plantation, someone has to be alert to the moment when the plan doesn't work. When this happens everything must stop and the process must be rethought. The necessary changes can be costly. Often such incidents are no one person's fault. So many people are responsible for a job as big as the Rosedown project, mistakes can be the result of bad communication or failure to coordinate the many aspects of the job. Hadley, with his keen sense of architectural detail, is ever vigilant in looking for potential problems.

One day I walked into one of the large parlors to discover an enormous air-conditioning vent that was soon to be installed. I don't know anything about air-conditioning but I knew the vent was ugly. I asked the engineer why we were using it. He responded that this was the standard size vent for the duct that would supply the air needed for the room. When I asked if it had to be that shape, he said no. I insisted that new designs for the vent be developed. Vents that fit above the crown moldings were custom-made for all of the rooms. After they were installed, the vents were not visible.

Revealing his love of functional unity, when Hadley recalled the Rosedown project in *Sixty Years of Interior Design: The World of McMillen*, Hadley said: "The thing I like so much about Rosedown was the unity of the project. There was the land being restored to grazing, the gardens being brought under control, the house being restored for family life. It was an historic house but it was also a domestic house."

The Rosedown Plantation project extended over the entire time that I worked at McMillen. In fact, I remained with the firm a year longer than I intended so that I could honor a promise that I made to Mr. Underwood. On one of my many trips to St. Francisville, Mr. Underwood took me aside and said, "Albert, promise me one thing—that every day you will do at least one thing that adds to finishing the work here." I kept my word. When I left McMillen in 1961, Rosedown Plantation was complete.

ABOVE
Final sketch for Rosedown breakfast room

RIGHT
Formal dining room at Rosedown

While Rosedown was the biggest project that Hadley worked on during his five years at McMillen, Inc., he had many other projects that brought him great satisfaction.

On several occasions Mrs. Brown asked me to assist on the decorating commissions that she handled personally. I worked with her when she decorated the main rooms of the Knickerbocker Club at Sixty-second Street and Fifth Avenue and when she redecorated the River Club at River House on East Fifty-second Street. She was a professional through and through. Shopping with her and observing her work with the committees at the clubs was a fantastic opportunity.

When the Williamsburg Inn was built in Williamsburg, Virginia, McMillen was commissioned to do the interior design. In addition to the public rooms and dining rooms, we did all of the guest bedrooms and

Hadley sketch for Rosedown bedroom and photo of the finished room

suites. For these, we developed five different schemes that were repeated throughout the inn. The finished work was a huge success and brought the firm a great deal of publicity.

Soon after this work was completed, the directors of the Williamsburg Foundation again called on McMillen. This time the commission was to decorate the Golden Horseshoe, a private club in the basement of the inn. Because that part of Virginia was dry, meaning no alcohol was served in public places, the bar was called a private club. Any guest checking into the inn was asked to join for a membership fee of one dollar. Mrs. Brown assigned the project to Miss Fakes. I was her front man and project manager.

When we were told that horseshoes must be boldly displayed in the decorative scheme, Miss Fakes worked her design magic. She would never do anything so obvious as hang horseshoes over the doors or on the walls. In her mind, horseshoes belonged on the floor. Creating a fascinating design, she had gilded horseshoes embedded into the floor, which was then glazed a brilliant red. The effect was terrific and the board members of the Williamsburg Inn loved it. Working with Miss Fakes instilled in me the absolute importance of details in any decorating job.

Following Mrs. Brown's lead, the decorators at McMillen produced very traditional schemes, which was the style throughout the fifties. As we approached the sixties, lifestyles became less formal and decorating began to change. Natalie Davenport was the one senior decorator who was adventuresome and open to the lifestyle changes. Shopping with her was a terrific experience—she never tired of looking for new and different things. Natalie was also great about sharing ideas. When I was assisting her on a project for Gregory B. Smith, he suggested that we decorate his apartment as though it were in Paris. The apartment lent itself perfectly to his idea. Located in the building that had been the private home of Joseph Pulitzer, it had extraordinary high ceilings and magnificent belle époque doors and windows. I had the idea of redesigning the bedroom, changing the shape from a square into an octagon and covering all of the walls with fabric. Natalie went along with the plan and Mr. Smith was delighted.

One of my first big breaks came one evening at a friend's apartment when I had the good fortune to meet the great stage and film director Josh Logan and his wife, Nedda. The Logans had just returned from a trip to Paris, where they bought a lot of things from the great French decorator Madeleine Castaing. They talked about needing a decorator to create a suitable background in their bedroom for these new purchases and their other Napoleon III furniture. As the party was breaking up and we were leaving, Nedda asked me if I would be willing to work with her and Josh.

The next morning when I reported all of this to Mrs. Brown, she was quite surprised. Working on the Josh Logan apartment in River House was a pretty big assignment. After seeing the things they bought in Paris and their other French antiques, I developed my plan. A pink-and-white, floral-and-ribbon strip fabric would be used for the wall covering. For the large windows that faced the East River, I designed soft draped curtains,

*to be made of the same fabric that I used on
the walls, with embroidered Swiss sheer
undercurtains. On the upholstered furniture
and pillows I used several floral prints. The
rug was a deep green with a tiny pink rose-
bud design. The scheme was very romantic.
On the day I was scheduled to make my
presentation to the Logans, I gathered my
fabric samples, color swatches, and sketches
and headed off to River House.*

*As I was leaving the office, Mrs. Brown
asked to see what I was taking. When I presented my scheme to her, she said, "But
Hadley, you have only one plan. There are
no choices." I said I knew what the Logans
wanted and this was all that I intended to
show. I believed then, and still do, that
showing a client too much is confusing.
Seeing that I had amplified their Paris purchases in my scheme, Josh and Nedda were
totally pleased and accepted the proposal
without any alterations.*

Even though Hadley was working in a firm
where all of the decorators' work reflected the taste and style of the
owner, Eleanor Brown, he was forming his own opinions and ways of
working, and, as in the case of the Joshua Logan commission, he was putting them to use.

Natalie Davenport

*Decorators should always remember that letting a client see too many beau-
tiful things is a pitfall. I have always believed that the more educated the
clients are, the easier they are to work with. Clients with a knowledge of decorating, and an ability to articulate what they want from the finished project, make the designer's job easier. The Logans were a perfect example of this.*

*One day a smartly dressed woman came into the McMillen offices
and said that she was interested in talking with one of the designers
about decorating a new house that she and her husband were building.
At McMillen we seldom, if ever, had people come in without an appointment. There was no way that someone could just walk in off the street
and see Mrs. Brown or one of the senior decorators. As the low man on
the totem pole, I was called to meet the visitor.*

*She was stunningly dressed in all black—black dress, black shoes,
and pocketbook. Her only piece of jewelry was a large gold pendant sus-
pended on a gold necklace. The pendant, shaped like a carnival mask,
had pierced eyes that appeared to move as the pendant moved freely over
the upper bodice of her black dress. She was also wearing a black hat
with a sheer black veil that was pulled away from her face, and her hair
was jet black. After an introduction and the usual pleasantries of*

meeting someone, she said that she and her husband were building a house in Dallas. Remembering the branch office of McMillen that was in Houston from 1940 until 1943, the woman and her husband hoped that someone from our firm would work with them and their architect. She was very clear about what she wanted—a small house in the neoclassical style with Louis XVI interior details and furnishings. I agreed to go to Dallas and meet her husband for an initial interview.

Several days later, armed with a copy of The Small Houses and Gardens of Versailles, I headed west. At our first meeting, I was introduced to the architect and the landscape designer. Clearly the clients' object was to create a harmonious ambiance that flowed from the house into the gardens. Working with them and their western team was a delightful experience and the house turned out to be a little jewel. The success of the project proves the point that we never know when a glorious opportunity will walk through the door—often without an appointment.

Even though Hadley was getting his own clients, such as the Logans and his Texas commission, decorators were not paid a lot of money in those days. It was still necessary for him to take on other work. A moonlighting job that he got through his friend Reneé Meyers proved to be more than a source for extra money—Hadley would at last be a real fashion designer.

One of my best friends at McMillen was Reneé Meyers, the secretary for Marion Morgan. Once when Reneé was invited to a dinner dance, she asked me to design her dress. Her escort was a man who owned a Seventh Avenue sportswear company. When he saw Reneé's dress, he asked if she thought I would be interested in moonlighting, doing freelance designs for his firm. Of course I was interested, and for several months I went to his loft on Saturday mornings and worked on designs. My specific assignment was to design lower-priced dresses for the company's Shoestring Collection. I knew nothing about sewing but I would cut the fabric as I wanted, pin it to a dress form, and leave it for the pattern makers. The only one of my designs that I know was produced was a ladies belt that was marketed as The Twenty-eight-inch Waist. It was nothing more than a flexible tape measure cut to twenty-eight inches with a buckle. All over New York City I saw women wearing "my" belt.

I can honestly say I had a very good time working at McMillen. The firm's distinguished clients and prestigious reputation was the result of one woman's vision—Eleanor Brown.

Mrs. Brown was very firm in how she wanted things done at McMillen. Her business training was apparent in every facet of the operation. One of her strict observances was office hours. Everyone was expected to be at work by nine o'clock sharp and the offices closed promptly at five. She believed that something was wrong if a person could not get his or her work done in these hours. We were not allowed to come into the offices on Saturday or Sunday.

Every day at four o'clock we had afternoon tea. The maid rolled a mahogany cart from office to office and we were served tea and cookies in

Hadley fashion sketch

English china cups and plates: no paper cups at McMillen. During the teatime ritual, Mrs. Brown had an individual chat with each decorator. She wore heavy gold bracelets that jangled while she made her rounds. Hearing her bracelets, we knew when she was on her way. She used her time with us to edit our work and to get an update on the status of our projects.

In 1982, in *Sixty Years of Interior Design: The World of McMillen*, Hadley said, "Until Eleanor came along the lady decorators were doing pretty, comfy houses without much direction or point of view. It was her strong design consciousness that made McMillen different. She had an educated eye, an educated mind, and she worked relentlessly to achieve perfection and beauty. Also, I think Eleanor was ahead of her time in her sense of adventure in bringing things together that were totally compatible but not of the same period. I think it was a return to almost neoclassical attitudes.

"Her own personal taste was always for the late eighteenth-century and for classical, formal, symmetrical interiors. There [was] an enormous sense of order about what she [did] but it [was] relaxed; things [weren't] always placed in pairs. She [had] a very intellectual sense, not just about color and texture, but about the ability and function of things. There's no nonsense. Her fanciful side shows in other ways, through modern pictures and modern sculpture. The contemporary aspect of her work comes not so much through furniture but through the things that one brings to a well-organized space."

My experience with Mrs. Brown and the other decorators at McMillen was a formative five years in my life. I was the only male decorator on the staff. The professional aspects of decorating were drummed into me along with a very clear understanding of quality goods, dependable suppliers, and reliable craftsmen and artisans. Mrs. Brown was unrelenting in her insistence that a good decorator must know what resources are available and where the most suitable goods can be found.

At the same time that Hadley was learning the business of the decorating trade at McMillen, Inc., he was also getting to know a group of very talented New Yorkers.

The apartment that Wilbur Pippin and I leased was a duplex. We had the ground floor and the basement, which opened onto a garden. It was on East Fifty-eighth Street, adjacent to the ramp that leads to the Queensboro Bridge. A tall garden wall completely closed out the sound of the traffic. I painted the floor of the entrance hall a brilliant red. The walls were white there, as they were in every room. Reminiscent of portieres, I hung large-scale, black-and-white check curtains that divided the hall. In the sitting room I hung the pink sheer China silk curtains from my apartment on Fifty-seventh Street. On the upholstered furniture I used cotton fabrics that were either solid black or white. The major piece of furniture in the room was an eighteenth-century Italian console.

At the same time that we moved into the Fifty-eighth Street apartment, Billy Baldwin was decorating Cole Porter's cottage in Williamstown, Massachusetts. One afternoon Billy telephoned, very excited about an eighteenth-century Italian chandelier that he had seen in an antiques shop. The next day Wilbur and I drove up to Williamstown and bought the chandelier. It was so large that it barely fit into the car. The carved wooden center post, wire arms, and carved wooden bobeches were painted Venetian blue with gold trim. I must say it gave grand style to the sitting room.

Wilbur had been trained as a photographer, and he was a very good one, but when we moved into the duplex, he was working in public relations for the New York City Ballet. His idea of fun was to have the apartment full of people, which meant that we were constantly entertaining. Wilbur enjoyed doing all of the cooking and I did the cleaning up, which I hated. I have never had any interest in domestic chores and food holds no fascination for me.

Hadley fashion sketch

Through his work Pippin had many connections in the art world. George Balanchine and his wife, Tanaquil LeClerq, Lincoln Kirstein, George Platt Lynes, Monroe Wheeler, Glenway Wescott, and Paul Cadmus were all frequent guests at the apartment. On occasion, Geraldine Stutz, the president of Henri Bendel, commissioned Pippin to do freelance photography. At the time, Andy Warhol was doing illustrations for Bendel's shoe advertisements. When Pippin found out that Warhol and his mother were neighbors, he wasted no time in inviting them for dinner.

The line of Wilbur's friends that were constantly in and out of the apartment was never ending. I remember one evening when I stood before a sink stacked with dirty plates, glasses, knives, forks, and pots and pans that I had to wash and dry, a great sadness came over me. I thought, "What have I gotten myself into?" I was not really interested in these people and had little to say to them. Often I would leave and have dinner alone. I learned a big lesson during those years: I did not want to live with another person. In such arrangements there is little chance for the quiet times that are important to me.

During the last year of our lease, Wilbur's public relations work was extremely demanding and he became seriously ill. After months of bed rest, I encouraged him to rent a studio and return to his photography. I also commissioned him to photograph the leading New York interior designers. Many of his portraits are in this book. He was terrific at photographing interiors. Through our friend, Carrie Donovan, who was the home furnishings editor at the New York Times, *he immediately got a lot of work.*

One of the big breaks that Hadley got in his years at McMillen, Inc. was having his work published in a leading shelter magazine. It would be the beginning of his many features from important editors.

In 1959 Allison Bisgood, the decorating editor at Vogue, *asked me to design a room for a feature story, "Summer on a Shoestring—Before and After." I was to show on one page the typical drab room that one might find in a summer rental. On the opposite page I was to show how the room could be decorated without spending a lot of money. My design made a hit with Allison and I got my first big publicity—a double-page, color spread in* House & Garden.

During my fourth year with McMillen, 1960, I celebrated my fortieth birthday. That year Mrs. Polly Jessup wrote and asked me to join her staff in Palm Beach as a senior decorator. A large firm in Amarillo, Texas, also contacted me about a senior position with them. Neither offer interested me. In addition to my work at McMillen, I was moonlighting at the fabric house, Arthur H. Lee. My job was to recolor and restyle fabrics from their archives. They liked my work and later asked me to design a complete line of new fabrics.

Early in 1961 Mrs. Brown arranged for an exhibition of room portraits by Elizabeth Hoops, an artist who had done work for McMillen over the years. The exhibit, which was held in our showrooms, got terrific reviews. Elizabeth Hoops had an amazing technique with watercolors and gouache. When she painted a room, the fabric patterns and textures were readily recognizable and yet she did not work in a harsh realistic style. Her room renderings had a romantic softness and allure.

When the show opened, Mrs. Brown was interviewed by the New York Times. *In the* Times *article she made the statement that women are better decorators than men. What she said didn't really surprise me. On more than one occasion she had said she didn't think much of the work of Billy Baldwin or Bill Pahlmann. When I read the article, I was both hurt and angry. It is one thing to have harsh judgments and talk about them. It is quite another thing to have them printed in the* New York Times. *I waited several days, to cool down and gain my composure before approaching Mrs. Brown about her comment.*

One morning Mrs. Brown and I were on the back stairs at McMillen—just the two of us—and I seized the moment. I said to her that if she really believed what she had said in the Times, *it left me little choice but to resign. Mrs. Brown's response was, "Oh come, come,*

Hadley, you're too sensitive. Just calm down and get over it." The following morning she called me into her office and said, "Hadley, I've been thinking about your comment yesterday and if you really feel that way then perhaps it is better for you to resign."

Mrs. Brown was always a businesswoman. One of the first rules in business is to never try to change the mind of a person who offers his or her resignation. When a person resigns, accept his or her resignation and work out an appropriate termination. Certainly this is the policy I have always followed. Mrs. Brown and I worked out a suitable time for my departure and I stayed with McMillen until the end of the year. I finished every project that I was working on and honored my promise to Mr. Underwood that I would not leave the firm until Rosedown was finished.

After work on the day that Mrs. Brown accepted my resignation and we had worked out the termination agreement, I called Van Truex to tell him what had happened. I wanted him to hear the news from me and not through the decorator grapevine. I also wanted him to know

Wilbur Pippin

that Mrs. Brown and I had parted on the best of terms. This would be important to him since Eleanor Brown was one of his closest friends and had been on the Board of Trustees at Parsons during the years that he was president.

One of Hadley's many gifts is his sense of timing. Another is his indomitable courage to do what he thinks is right. He had to have had some anxiety the day that Mrs. Brown accepted his resignation. He was over forty years old and had yet to build up any financial security. His mettle to stand firm, even with his employer, led to the biggest opportunity in his life.

The following morning, my phone rang soon after seven. It was Van. He didn't even say "Hello" or introduce himself. He blurted out, "Do you know who I mean when I say Sister Parish?" I assured him that I did. I reminded him that he had introduced me to Mrs. Parish in the china department at Tiffany's when she and Mrs. Brown were each arranging a tabletop display for one of the company's Decorator Tables shows.

Van went on to say, "Last night I sat next to Sister Parish at a dinner party and she told me that unless she could find someone to help with her work, she was thinking about going out of business. I told her that I would have you call her. Call her this morning soon after eight o'clock."

When I called Mrs. Parish, she answered the phone. I introduced myself and said that Van had told me to call. In our brief conversation, a time was set for our first meeting.

Hadley's first major publicity,
"Summer on a Shoestring,"
designed for a feature in Vogue,
showing before, left and bottom
left, and after, bottom right and
facing page

A Fine Romance

PRECEDING PAGES
New "York Rose"

Albert Hadley was forty-two years old when he began his new job. Mrs. Parish, known as Sister Parish, was fifty-two. She was well established in her business that catered to the upper crust of old-money society. At the time that Hadley joined her, Mrs. Parish was completing her work at the White House for President and Mrs. John F. Kennedy and had a growing international reputation.

I was nervous when I went for my job interview with Mrs. Parish. When I was first introduced to her at Tiffany's, Mrs. Parish barely paused from her work and her only response was a polite but distant, "It is nice to meet you, Mr. Hadley." With this memory of her, at the appointed late-afternoon hour, in October 1961, I rang the doorbell of the Parishes's apartment on East Seventy-ninth Street.

In her stockinged feet, Mrs. Parish opened the door. Her spiteful little Pekingese, Yummy, came flying at me. After inviting me in, as she turned to lead the way into her sitting room, she said, "Would you zip me up." I reached forward and zipped up the back of her black wool dress. And that is how it all began.

I followed her into the room. She sat comfortably on the sofa and said, "Before you sit down, why don't you mix us a drink." Pointing to the drinks tray, she said "I'll have bourbon." I mixed what I thought was a reasonable drink of bourbon and water. When I handed it to Mrs. Parish, she took a sip and said, "You call this a drink?" She handed it back to me and said "Bourbon. Just bourbon and some ice." When she took a sip of the bourbon on the rocks, her only reply was, "That's better." I remember thinking that she looked absolutely ravishing.

Even though I was nervous and intimidated by her manner, I liked her and I could tell that she liked me. Three days later she called to say that she would like me to work with her. We agreed that I would start in early January 1962.

Mrs. Parish's office was on East Sixty-ninth Street, just off Madison Avenue. She had one assistant, Richard Nelson, and a secretary and a maid. During Hadley's first year, Nelson resigned to open his own firm in Newport, Rhode Island. Two years later, in 1964, Hadley and Mrs. Parish formed a partnership, Parish-Hadley, Inc.

Hadley with Sister Parish

Looking back, I always say that in Nashville, A. Herbert Rodgers started me on my course—he opened doors. Mrs. Brown taught me the business aspects of interior design. And Sis introduced me to the world of the socially elite. During my first year with her we worked on commissions for President and Mrs. Kennedy on the White House, Mrs. Robert Charles, then Oatsie Leiter, the doyen of Washington and Newport society, Mr. and Mrs. Edgar Bronfman, and Mrs. Vincent Astor.

Tuesday, January 2, 1962, was the date that Sis told me to report for work. On Monday, January 1, my telephone rang soon after eight o'clock in the morning. Without any greeting, such as good morning or happy new year, Mrs. Parish said, "This is Mrs. Henry Parish. I thought we could get an early start. I would like to show you the Edgar Bronfman apartment. Meet me at 740 Park Avenue at noon."

Mrs. Parish had recently agreed to decorate an enormous apartment at 740 for Edgar Bronfman, the chairman of Seagram, and his wife, Ann Loeb. The apartment had been the New York residence of Electra Havemeyer Webb, the founder of the Shelburne Museum in Shelburne, Vermont. Mrs. Parish envisioned the rooms in a traditional scheme using her signature floral chintz. Since this was the first job I would be doing with her, I listened to her ideas, took notes, and offered opinions only when I was asked.

The apartment was enormous, typical of the spaces in luxury pre-war buildings. The rooms had high ceilings, elaborate moldings, and doors and large windows that provided beautiful views and abundant light. After an hour or so in the empty apartment, Mrs. Parish went on to a New Year's Day party and I went to lunch with Miss Rose Cumming. About a week later, when we were well into the project, we received a telegram from the Bronfmans who were in Mexico. "Stop all work until we return. We want a floating apartment." Mrs. Parish looked at me and said, "What in God's name do they mean by a 'floating apartment?'" I knew exactly what they wanted: they wanted a modern apartment with lots of

Hadley sketch for President John F.
Kennedy's breakfast room at the
White House

clean, uncluttered spaces. When I told this to Sis, her response was a dis-
gusted "Ugh." As soon as the Bronfmans returned from Mexico, Sis and
I met with them to discuss the "floating" apartment.

Sis had very little interest in changing the architectural background
of a house or an apartment when I started working for her. On the other
hand, I had been trained at McMillen to make whatever alterations were
necessary to achieve the desired effect in any project. I also kept notes,
made sketches and drawings, and worked with a plan. Working with the
architect, Jack Cobel, I immediately went to work helping to design the
apartment. To achieve the look that the Bronfmans wanted meant gut-
ting the apartment and starting over. You cannot make a modern apart-
ment out of a traditional space. After the demolition, an enormous
amount of construction was done before any decorating could begin. To
create a sculptural space, entire walls were removed and replaced with
glass. My plans included the installation of a freestanding curving
travertine-marble staircase.

Once Sis got over the initial shock of what was required, she went back to the things she liked doing most—shopping for a collection of important eighteenth-century furniture and designing curtains. Sis called anything made of fabric that hung at a window "curtains." The words draperies or window treatments were not in her vocabulary. Somehow everything she did worked in the modern space. The antique chairs became like pieces of sculpture and the apartment was fantastic.

When our work was finished, the Bronfmans were delighted. Leaving the elevator, you stepped into a mirrored foyer—not just flat mirrors but delineated and beveled-edge mirrors—floor to ceiling. The heavy green lacquered doors, opening from this space into the hall, were ten feet tall and five feet wide with custom hardware that was made by an artisan who was a friend of Mrs. Parish. Identical doors were installed on the opposite wall. The wooden floors were removed and were replaced with travertine marble. Mrs. Parish had never done anything like this. The project became a big turning point in her thought process. I could never have done what I did without Sis and she couldn't have done what she did without me.

My first work for Mrs. Vincent Astor was on her house in Northeast Harbor, Maine. This project was started during my first year with Sis. We worked together on the plans and schemes but I was definitely the

Hadley sketch for the crèche figures used by Mrs. Kennedy at the White House

GOLDEN PAPER MACHE FIGURES
CREATE A FACELESS NATIVITY FOR THE WHITE HOUSE
CHRISTMAS 1964

assistant. With Brooke Astor giving her approval to every detail, the job proceeded. Sis and I worked closely with her on the paint colors and wall finishes, discussing at length every aspect of the job. The work was done during the winter so that the house would be ready for Brooke to move into that summer, "the season." As I had been trained at Parsons and as we worked at McMillen, I planned on paper where each piece of furniture was to be placed. In my head I knew exactly how the finished project would look. Little did I know!

On the day that everything—furniture, rugs, tables, lamps, and curtains—was scheduled to arrive in Northeast Harbor, Sis and I drove up from the Parishes's house in Dark Harbor, Maine, to meet the truck coming from New York City. It was all very exciting. As the truck was being unloaded, I got out my plans and began directing the workmen about the placement of the things in the house. When Sis saw what I was doing, she immediately took over. My plans went by the way. In her inimitable way Sis was pushing things around: "These chairs over there . . . this sofa here . . . put that lamp here. This goes there and that goes into another room." Well, that's the way she worked. She had a gift for arrangement, for putting things in the perfect place, and her attitude was always: "Forget the floor plans. Arrange the furniture where it is the most comfortable and will look best." When the work was finished and everything in place, it was perfection. That was Sis's magic. Brooke was very happy and that was the point of the whole thing. The most important part! Brooke's Northeast Harbor house was the beginning of my understanding of Sister Parish and my devotion to her.

From the beginning, in an odd way, Sis and I loved each other. This is not to say we did not have our trying moments; we did. There was a time when I wasn't sure I could last under the pressure of working with her. Sis could be very difficult and self-centered, caring only about herself and her own work. The two things that saved the relationship were that we were completely different and we had the utmost respect and admiration for each other. Sis couldn't help being a snob; her background made her that way. Having grown up in a world of privilege, it was her nature to be cautious. Sis's family and friends meant more to her than anything. She was extremely private, slow to speak, controlled, and very cautious about spending money. Mark Hampton, who worked for us, said that her strong self-assurance came from the good fortune of being born into a distinguished family with plenty of money, having three adoring brothers (hence her nickname Sister), and her unmistakable taste.

In contrast to Sis and her world of privilege, Mrs. Brown was a Midwesterner who made no attempt to be a part of New York society or the eastern establishment. While she had wealthy clients from the upper echelon, Mrs. Brown kept her dealings with them on a strictly business basis. Unlike Sis, she would never advise clients on their children or their dogs. In a way Mrs. Brown was very cold where Sis, even with her snobby ways, was warm and loving. The two women had very little use for each other. Whenever they met in the elevator of the D & D building, Mrs. Brown would ask, "Still in trade, Sister?" Sis in a chilling tone of voice would sim-

PARISH-HADLEY

ply reply, "Of course I am." Sis was saddled with the memory that after she and Henry Parish II, were married, her mother had Mrs. Brown decorate their first New York residence.

With Sis, decorating was done in her head; nothing was written down. At McMillen, clients were presented with a scheme, an estimate of the costs, and a projected work schedule. Sis kept no records, gave no estimates, and did everything based on a sense of trust. Since most of the people she worked for were her friends, she would show them some fabric samples and tell them what she planned to do. If they liked it, she did it.

When I arrived, there was no filing system and no record of income and expenses. Receipts were tucked in envelopes with no particular order. Client memos and orders were jotted down on notepads but there was no organization. When I asked Sis if she would mind my having a friend set up a bookkeeping and accounting system, she said it would be fine with her. With Mrs. Brown's permission, her bookkeeper, Martha Snyder, worked for us in the evening establishing our mode of business.

Mrs. Henry Parish II

Further reflecting on their years together, Hadley said, "We had our differences and they were often enormous. We fought a lot. We loved a lot. We complemented each other. We were always on the same wavelength. Even though our styles were different, we had the same philosophy about our work. We had a wonderful, wonderful life together, a wonderful time." Before her death, forty years later, Mrs. Parish recalled: "We fight a lot, but we complement each other. It's an interesting balance."

Their corporation, Parish-Hadley, Inc., would become legendary in the annals of interior design. The success of Parish-Hadley, Inc. is concrete evidence that opposites do attract.

Mrs. Parish was unabashedly devoted to a luxurious, old-world, comfortable look that was first promoted by Sybil Colefax, John Fowler, and Nancy Lancaster in London. Her decorating signature was big floral chintz, down cushions, pattern on pattern, and rooms filled with beautiful but unpretentious things. "Deep downy upholstery is absolutely what

Detail of the fireplace in the apartment that Hadley designed for Robert Yoh

I've always been about," said Mrs. Parish when she described her work. The late Mark Hampton, who worked at Parish-Hadley before going on to become one of the leading decorators in New York, said, "Mrs. Parish thinks it's bad manners for a room to look pretentious." According to Nancy Novogrod, a former editor of *HG*, as *House & Garden* was called in the eighties, Mrs. Parish was totally responsible for the American country-house look that took America by storm when pictures of the interior of her house in Maine were published. She did all of her decorating without a day of training. Her skill and great taste came from the way she was brought up and lived. Hadley said, "I always dreamed of being in the world that Sis came from and lived in all of her life."

In dramatic contrast to Mrs. Parish, Hadley graduated from Parsons School of Design and taught there for five years. His knowledge of interior design is encyclopedic. The dictums of his teacher, Van Day Truex, still define his standard of taste. The simple, unadorned style of Truex, Jean-Michel Frank, and Billy Baldwin is ever present in Hadley's approach to design. While he fully understands luxury and is fascinated by fashion and glamour, the rooms he creates are not about money and expense, they are the essence of understated style and simplicity. An eclectic mix of fabrics, textures, colors, furniture, and accessories, first nurtured by Rose Cumming and displayed in William Pahlmann's over-the-top rooms at Lord & Taylor, is ever present in Hadley's work. He confesses that the "spirit, wit and style" of Elsie de Wolfe, Dorothy Draper, Syrie Maugham, and Ruby Ross Wood are guiding forces in his decorating. When he talks about design, Hadley frequently refers to the work of the Mexican architect Luis Barragán. One of his favorite Barragán quotes is from the architect's acceptance speech when he was awarded the Pritzker Prize: "It is alarming that publications devoted to [design] have banished from their pages the words beauty, inspiration, magic, spellbound, enchantment, as well as the concepts of serenity, silence, intimacy, and amazement . . . they have never ceased to be my guiding lights." Certainly this is also true of Hadley.

In *The Life and Works of Luis Barragán*, the architect says, "Memories of my father's [farm] underlie all my work, and my work feeds on transposing these distant, nostalgic longings to the contemporary world."[4]

Again, Barragán's words ring true for Hadley. Living in a rural environment during his formative years instilled in him the simple elegance and beauty found in nature. His mentor, Van Truex, also a man who spent his early years on a farm, held firm that "Nature is our best teacher."

Even with their divergent backgrounds and different design aesthetic, the partnership of Hadley and Mrs. Parish flourished and their work made design history. William Hodgins, a former assistant at Parish-Hadley, Inc., and now the leading decorator in Boston, said, "I've always thought that either of them was better than anyone else. But together!" They produced custom-designed furniture, wallpaper, and fabrics; did inspired geometric patterns on stained and painted floors; and were the first to use American crafts in upscale decorating, including patchwork quilts, rag rugs, hand-woven bedspreads, handmade baskets, and knitted throws.

During the first ten years that Hadley and Mrs. Parish worked together, the United States was fraught with anger and violence. These years were marked by the Vietnam War. Antiwar protests closed the campuses of Columbia and Harvard universities. Riots, demonstrations, and death occurred in every major city. The world witnessed the assassinations of President John Kennedy, his brother, Senator Robert Kennedy, and Dr. Martin Luther King, Jr. A cultural revolution was happening in America as values and morals underwent a profound shift.

For people in the decorative arts and home furnishings business, specifically interior design, the cultural revolution of the sixties signaled the arrival of pop art. Many decorators were excited by the designs that emerged from the new art and employed them in fabrics, wall coverings, furniture design, and lighting. For their clients, Hadley and Mrs. Parish held firm to their decorating mantra, defined by Hadley as the "chic of suitability."

Even with her insistence on the old-world look of elegance and comfort for our clients, Sis could be quite daring in things that she did for herself. In 1970, when pop and op art were seen everywhere in the decorative arts—in fabrics, wall coverings, and furniture design—Sis decided that her own apartment needed a new look. I was asked to scheme the job but she said she didn't want to get rid of one piece of furniture. All of Sis's things were antiques and very ornate, which meant the new look would have to be achieved in the background. I covered the walls in an egg-plant-colored vinyl. At the windows, I used silver metal blinds and pink curtains that were made out of a cotton fabric that we designed for Lee Jofa. Alan Campbell designed the fabric for the pillows and some of the chairs. A large dhurrie rug covered most of the floor. Sis's eclectic mix of furniture was great in the room and the modern look amplified her keen interest in the new things that were happening in the world.

Even though Sis gave the impression of being overly formal, she had a humorous, light side. Her great spirit and zest was most evident in her Sunday-night parties. Each week as she went about town, talking with friends, meeting people here and there, she would say, "Come over Sunday evening. I'm having a few people in." She never kept track of who

she invited or how many people were coming. When Sunday evening arrived, her guests were pleasantly packed into her apartment and everyone had a terrific time.

Sis was very fond of Halston, the fashion designer, who was frequently invited to her Sunday evenings. He always wore the same outfit: black turtleneck sweater, black trousers, black shoes and socks. When Sis asked him why he dressed that way, he replied, "Every time I get dressed I pretend I'm Babe Paley." Sis loved outrageous remarks but did not tolerate ribald language. She was crazy about Andy Warhol, who often showed up with an entourage of strange people. I never knew why Sis invited him. Warhol and his group would stand around looking very bored and never said a word.

Even though Sis always had fun at her parties, she never lost control—of anything. I remember one evening when a maid, who was assisting in the kitchen, put a thin layer of cheese spread on some Ritz crackers and then topped each one with a perfect slice of stuffed green olive. When Sis saw the hors d'oeuvres, she said, "Get those olive slices off; I hate decorated food. And pile the cheese on; no thin spreading." Sis wanted food to look appetizing and simple.

PRECEDING PAGES
Hadley-designed apartment for Robert Yoh featuring tin palm trees from a Harlem nightclub

The list of successful decorators who came to Parish-Hadley, Inc. as assistants, and after sufficient tutelage under Hadley and Mrs. Parish left to form their own firms, reads like a Who's Who in American interior design. In addition to the prominent Boston designer William Hodgins, the Parish-Hadley staff has included Pamela Banker, Libby Cameron, David Anthony Easton, Mariette Himes Gomez, Joanne de Guardiola, Keith Irvine, Thomas Jayne, David Kleinberg, Brian McCarthy, Kevin McNamara, Brian Murphy, Nicholas Miles Pentecost, Harold Simmons, Bunny Williams, and the late Tice Alexander, Gary Hager, Mark Hampton, and Robert Yoh. At one time the Parish-Hadley staff totaled more than twenty-five people, including their own architectural design department headed by David McMahon.

As our business expanded and we hired other decorators, Sis had problems dealing with the young people on our staff, especially the women. If one of the girls, as she called them, came into the office wearing an outfit Sis didn't approve of or had her hair cut in a way that Sis didn't like, she told her very bluntly. One of the women who started with us soon after she came to New York has told me that she will never forget Sis's stern rebukes. After receiving harsh words from Sis, the young assistant would go to her office and sob. Now, years later, she says it wasn't always easy to take but she always learned from Sis's criticism.

While Sis was nicer to the young men on our staff, she could be very critical when one of them did something that didn't suit her. I remember once buying a large gold pinkie ring. My small hands and fingers made the ring appear enormous. I thought it looked great since my friend Van Truex wore a gold pinkie ring that had been made for him by Millicent Rogers. The first day I wore my new ring in the office, Mrs. Parish looked at it and said, "What is that?" Her disdainful tone of voice let me know immediately that she did not approve. I never wore the ring again. Even with her demanding ways, I loved our years together and I miss her every day.

Each of our young decorators brought unique talents and spirit to Parish-Hadley. Some of them were with us for years; others stayed only a brief time and went on to other endeavors or opened their own firms. Mark Hampton was with us for only one summer before leaving to go to the London School of Economics; the following year he entered the New York University School of Fine Arts. Before Mark came for his job interview, Hilary Knight, the artist who created Eloise, called me and recommended him for a job.

I was always the one who met the prospective assistant designers. While I was interviewing them, Sis kept her office door open to hear what was said. While I was talking to Mark, Sis rang on the intercom and said, "I want to see this man before he leaves." As Mark and I were finishing our conversation, I asked him to stay and meet Mrs. Parish. She thought his voice and appearance reminded her of her late brother.

Hadley and Sister Parish in Moscow

Sis was always fond of Mark and when he and Duane invited us to their wedding in Solbury, Pennsylvania, there was no question about our accepting. Since the wedding was an evening affair, Sis wanted to leave the city early in the morning and do some antiquing on the way. She suggested that I dress casually and bring along a fresh shirt and tie. When I drove by to pick her up, Sis was in an informal outfit, carrying her dress on a hanger. As she got in the car, she said "I'll change later." After a busy day in and out of antiques shops, we got near Solbury. Sis asked me to pull the car over to the edge of the highway. She got out, taking her dress, and went behind the roadside bushes. As she made her way, she called over her shoulder, "Don't look." A few minutes later she emerged—looking her aristocratic best—dressed for the wedding.

Sis had a delightful way of springing surprises. I remember her calling me one evening and asking what I was doing for Thanksgiving. When I said I didn't have any definite plans she said, "Let's go to Ireland. We can do some shopping." That settled it. We were going to Ireland. On the day that we landed, as we were coming down the stairs from the plane, a beautiful burgundy-colored Rolls Royce arrived on the runway and pulled up to the side of the plane. A uniformed chauffeur got out, opened the door and who should emerge from the car but the great fashion designer Sybil Connolly. She came right over to us, gave Sis an embrace, introduced herself to me, and we all got into her Rolls and headed for our

hotel. Sis and Sybil talked about dresses all the way to Dublin. This was the first time I had heard anything about dresses and suddenly it became obvious that the real reason for our trip was for Sis to be fitted for custom suits and dresses at Sybil Connolly's boutique. I didn't really care why we made the trip. I had never been to Ireland and the idea of being there and shopping with Sis was thrilling.

Sis was always looking for new ideas. One day when we were in a country restaurant, Sis excused herself to go to the ladies' room. When she returned she was carrying an old dirty, tattered rug. In its better days it had been a primitive striped rag rug in an array of charming colors. Sis said we must ask the restaurant owner to sell us the rug so that we could have it reproduced in Ireland. When we asked if we could buy it, the man said, "Please, just take it." The rugs we had made were a great hit with our clients and over the years we used many versions of the design.

The one thing Sis and I had talked about buying in Ireland was baskets. One Sunday morning, on a trip we made to visit friends in the north, we spotted a sign on a barn that said Baskets. The barn was locked, so we went to the farmhouse, roused the owners, and asked to see their wares. Their assortment of beautiful handmade baskets was fantastic. We sold every one that we shipped back. The trip was such a success that for several summers after, Sis and Harry rented a house called Fort William, near Lismore Castle.

One of the most exciting adventures that Sis and I had was our trip to Moscow. In 1979 Thomas J. Watson, Jr., the former chairman of IBM, was appointed ambassador to the Soviet Union. Sis and I had done work for Tom and Olive Watson in Connecticut and at their house in Maine. Within ten days after the Watsons arrived in Moscow, they invited us to come and help arrange their furniture in the residence of the American embassy.

The year that we made the trip, Parish-Hadley employed a Polish man, Andrew Zaworcki, who drove our station wagon in New York. When I asked Andrew if my brown wool coat would be warm enough for the winter weather in Moscow, he said that he felt sure it would be. In the meantime, Elaine Court, a friend who was in the fashion business, wanted me to have a fur coat for the trip. I had no idea of going to a furrier, so Elaine had two coats sent to my apartment. I couldn't imagine wearing a fur coat and had them returned. On the day we were to fly out of New York, the weather was rather warm but Andrew said that he had heard that Russia was having a very cold winter and maybe I did need a fur coat. At the very last minute, he drove to Elaine's and brought back one of the coats. That night at the airport, when I took my fur coat out of the trunk of the car, Sis said she thought it looked ridiculous, I said, "Well, it's all I've got. Either I wear it or I don't go."

When we landed in Moscow and Olive saw me in the coat, she broke into giggles. She told us that Tom had wanted a fur coat but she couldn't stand the idea. One evening when the Watsons and Sis and I went to the Russian circus, a tiny brown bear came into the ring. The three of them—Sis, Olive, and Tom—broke into uncontrollable laughter and from then on, when I wore my fur coat, I was "Mr. Bear."

While I remember every job that Sis and I did with fondness, some bring back special memories. Once we were asked to consider decorating Estée and Joseph Lauder's house on the Upper East Side. Sis, Bill Hodgins, and I went to see the house. When we walked into the main drawing room, Sis looked at the massive stone chimneypiece and said, "I think that must be replaced." Mrs. Lauder said, "But Mrs. Parish, that is why we bought the house." From that moment on everything seemed to go wrong. As we were standing on the curving staircase, making our way to the second floor, Sis looked all around, up and down, and said, "Oh, what I could do with this house." Mrs. Lauder, who was on the step ahead of Sis, turned around, and with her thumb and forefinger, took Sis's chin and said, "Oh, what I could do with this face." Needless to say, we didn't get the job.

One morning, in the early sixties, our great friend Diana Vreeland called from the Metropolitan Museum and said there was a young man in her office whom she wanted Sis and me to meet. At Diana's suggestion, we invited him over. He was a very bright, young African-American minister from

Diana Vreeland

Selma, Alabama, who had organized a quilt-making cooperative for the women in his church. On the advice of Dr. Martin Luther King, Jr., he had come to New York to market the quilts. Sis and I were impressed with the workmanship and very much wanted to work with the women to produce hand-quilted fabrics. The young minister agreed for Jim Wagnon, a member of our staff, to go to Selma and assist with the financial arrangements.

The first time we used the quilted fabric was on a sofa for the William S. Paleys' house in Manhasset. It was so successful that we used another color combination and design for the curtains in the Washington dining room of Senator and Mrs. Charles Percy. The Percys' daughter, Sharon, was married to John D. Rockefeller, IV, who was then the governor of West Virginia. When Mrs. Rockefeller heard the story behind her mother's curtains, she set about to organize the same kind of quilting cooperatives in underdeveloped areas of West Virginia. The young Alabama preacher's courageous trip to New York City became a far-reaching ministry.

The People
Who Make it Happen

Many people who call themselves painters paint all of their lives and never sell any of their work. These people are still painters. Van Gogh is a perfect example. The same can be said of other creative people such as writers, composers, and sculptors, or craftspeople, such as potters. People who write but never have their work published can still be called writers. However, this is not true of interior decorators. To be a decorator, a person must have clients; without clients there is no decoration.

Mrs. Parish had rules about who she worked for and who she didn't. The rules weren't written down; like her decorating, she kept them in her head. A frequently told story about Mrs. Parish recalls that when she visited a house or apartment and knew on arrival that the job was not for her, she would say, "Albert, I am not feeling well. Please take me home." When the would-be client later called to inquire about Mrs. Parish's health and set up another appointment, the secretary was trained to say that Mrs. Parish indeed was not well and that the firm was not taking on any new work. That was the end of it.

It was always the policy of Parish-Hadley, Inc. never to give out the names of their clients unless they had allowed their names to be used when their houses were published. Among those who did allow this publicity were Bill and Babe Paley, Carter Burden, Mrs. Thomas Jefferson Coolidge, Annette de la Renta when she was married to Samuel Reed, Connie Mellon, Gordon and Ann Getty, Happy Rockefeller, and Louise Melhado, who has continued with the company as Louise Grunwald and was married to the late Henry Grunwald, the former editor-in-chief of Time, Inc. and the American ambassador to Austria. Certainly one of the firm's most celebrated commissions was working with Vice President and Mrs. Albert Gore.

While some of their clients were Mrs. Parish's longtime friends, many were not. But whenever Hadley and Mrs. Parish accepted a commission, the client could be assured of enjoying a caring relationship with both of them. Hadley and Mrs. Parish were frequently invited to their clients' homes for both small parties and gala events celebrating birthdays and anniversaries.

Hadley speaks warmly of these occasions and fondly remembers his personal experiences with clients. When talking about his times with Ambassador and Mrs. Henry Grunwald, he describes Louise Grunwald as one of the most terrific hostesses anywhere, who gives the best dinner parties and takes great delight in seeing that all of her guests have a good time: "Louise is a darling. I love her. She has the greatest wit and sense of fun. She has such chic—a magical way of doing things. In her houses the perfection is done with such ease, it's offhand in a way. It's so refreshing." When he talked about the work he and Mrs. Parish did for Oatsie Charles, he said, "Oatsie is terrific. How can you not like Oatsie? She has great style, taste, and lives in one of the most charming houses in Washington. She has a wonderful eye for furniture and objects. Her house is 'done' but 'not done.' It has a very relaxed quality."

The relationships that Mrs. Parish and Hadley developed with the clients lasted for years and often went from one generation to another. This kind of loyalty was deeply rooted in Mrs. Parish's background and upbringing. A good example is their ongoing work with the late Jane Engelhard and her daughter, Annette de la Renta.

When I came to work for Sis, Charles and Jane Engelhard were among her most loyal clients. Her first work for them was decorating their house in South Africa. She and Charles Engelhard had been childhood friends in Far Hills, and he had gone to St. Mark's, the Episcopal boarding school in Massachusetts, with her brothers. During the Parish-Hadley days we did work for the Engelhards in Far Hills, New York City, London, and Maine. Frequently the Parishes and I were invited to parties at Craigwood, their New Jersey estate. I remember thinking once that many of the people I had heard about, read about, or seen on television, and never dreamed of meeting, I met at Craigwood.

Every spring the Engelhards gave a fabulous party to honor the Duke and Duchess of Windsor, which they called The Royal Weekend. I had met the duchess at a benefit in New York but this was my first encounter with the duke. They were both charming and the duchess was much prettier than she appeared in photographs. She had the most beautiful complexion I had ever seen. When I sat next to her that evening she wanted to talk about nothing but interior decorating.

My first encounter with the Duchess of Windsor had been at the old Parke-Bernet Auction Gallery on Madison Avenue. Sis and I had done a

Sitting room in the country house
of Mr. and Mrs. Samuel Reed

model room there—a summer porch, really—for a charity benefit. The duchess was the honorary chairman of the event. This was long before the Kips Bay Show House was started. When the duchess came into our display, she admired a pair of planters that were made out of tree trunks. After she left, Sis said that whenever a member of the royal family admires something it is courteous to give it to them. That afternoon we had the planters wrapped and delivered to the Windsors' suite at the Waldorf-Astoria. When I saw the duchess again, at the Engelhards, she remembered that we had sent the planters to her and was extremely gracious in her gratitude.

Of all the famous and interesting people I met at the Engelhards, none was more captivating than Jane's daughter, Annette. I first knew her when she was a young bride, married to Samuel Reed. I did work for the Reeds in New York City, Katonah, New York, and Islesboro, Maine. I remember once, when Annette had gone with me to an upholstery workroom, she took a piece of fabric and after carefully folding and pleating it, she held it up, saying, "I think the pleats for the pillows should be like this." It has been remarkable to work with a young person with so much innate taste and style. Now Mrs. Oscar de la Renta, Annette remains a dear friend and as far as I'm concerned she has the greatest taste of any American woman of her generation.

Another family that I remember with great fondness is Mr. and Mrs. Leonard Davis. My first meeting with Mrs. Davis in 1967 took place in their relatively new apartment, which was in one of the first modern apartment buildings on Fifth Avenue. The spaces were agreeably furnished, comfortable, and appropriate, but somewhat lacking in personal style. The featured attraction was the panoramic view of Central Park that was afforded by an entire western wall of glass.

Sophie Davis was a charming woman of medium weight and build whose softly coiffed hair framed her animated and congenial face. Her costume was deceptively simple—flowing and comfortable.

After a few moments of introductory conversation, I was invited to look at the blueprints of the house that she and her husband were going to build in Palm Beach, Florida. The preliminary stages of planning with their architect, Milton Klein, had reached the point that the details for the interior had to be addressed.

I was fascinated by the design that I saw on paper—a strong monolithic facade of white stucco providing no indication of a rather open

120

plan beyond that it afforded dramatic visual access to the wide, sweeping expanse of green lawn that gave way to the distant ocean. The plan was intriguing: even though the house was major in scale and proportion, it contained only one bedroom—the nucleus of a vast master suite. In addition, there was a separate wing—two-storied—that consisted of guest accommodations.

No doubt my enthusiasm was obvious. After considerable conversation and study of the plans, Sophie Davis took me totally by surprise when she seriously asked, "Mr. Hadley, how much do you think that it will cost to furnish this house?" First of all, I was then, and still am, hopeless with budgets; everything always costs the sky! After a long moment, I finally said (my heart in my mouth), "Mrs. Davis, I would think, without antiques and artwork, that this is at least a million- dollar project." A long pause, and then, as a generous smile brightened her face, Mrs. Davis said, "I think you are about right; I'm glad that you don't underestimate." That, in a nutshell, is the beginning of the story of one of my most enjoyable and meaningful projects.

A few days later, Leonard Davis and his wife came to our modest but colorful and unorthodox street-level office on East Sixty-ninth Street, just off Madison Avenue toward Park Avenue. It was a very congenial first meeting and I have always felt that Mr. Davis, as well as Sophie, were amused as well as impressed by the informality and friendliness of our workplace.

The house was being built on property that had once been part of the Ogden Phipps Estate. To one side of the new structure was an impressive portion of the Phipps's celebrated gardens. There were statues and decorative architectural elements, including a wall fountain that fed a long, narrow reflecting pool. At this stage, the house itself promised to be as impressive, if not more so, than the design I had seen on paper.

Progress was made at the on-site meeting with Mr. and Mrs. Davis and their architect. This was but the first of many stimulating and creative adventures that we had while the house was being built.

Having seen the lay of the land, and the positioning of the house and its proximity to the old shaded garden, in as gentle a tone as I could muster, I asked about the reason for, and plan of, the proposed entrance to the property. The answer from the architect was perfectly logical—it was the most economical. I was looking at the placement of the house from another point of view.

My suggestion that the entrance to the grounds be made through the old gardens, taking full advantage of their magic and beauty, was met with great surprise and curiosity. I proceeded to describe the entry through decorative, welcoming gates—passing along a gently winding graveled surface through the luxuriant growth—approaching a wooden bridge that spanned the reflecting pool. The bridge would be constructed in a manner so that each passing wheel gave a soft rumbling signal. Farther along a wide bend brought one to a broad clearing giving a full view of the fabulous monolithic house. My case was won with enthusiasm.

Most of my work was, of course, done in New York: planning, scheming, and shopping for the furnishings for the new house. Sophie and I had

FACING PAGE
The Leonard Davis house, Palm Beach, Florida

LEFT
The entrance of the Leonard Davis House. Ancient Chinese horse heads on the right; in the garden is a large Henry Moore sculpture

ABOVE
Dining room

FOLLOWING PAGES
Vintage print of architectural detail in the Leonard Davis gardens. The property had originally been a part of the Phipps Estate.

*The large drawing room
of the Leonard Davis house*

FACING PAGE
*Detail of a guest sitting room,
the Leonard Davis house*

*scheduled weekly meetings to discuss plans and to make decisions. She
had a fantastic, strong point of view. When the time came to install the
furnishings in the new house, all was in readiness as truck after truck left
New York heading for Palm Beach.*

*As the job progressed, our meetings in Palm Beach became more fre-
quent. At one point, I think that the Davises became a bit anxious
because they were concerned that they just might be slightly off the
mark. It was at this time that Leonard said to me, at a late-night meeting, "Albert, what can I tell people, our friends, when they ask, 'What
kind of house are you building?' I can't say it's just a one-bedroom house
and I dare not tell them that there's a wing of guest rooms." I paused for
a moment and said, really without much thought, "Just say that you're
building a pavilion." His reply was, "Albert, what is a pavilion?" We*

made a joke of the whole thing. It wasn't until I sent him a copy of a recently published book, Pavilions of the Heart, *that my point was made. From that day on, the place that Leonard and Sophie Davis created and shared generously and lovingly in that spectacular seaside setting was forever a pavilion of the heart!*

At the same time that Sis and I were installing a large, light-filled room on the top floor of a town house on East Sixty-third Street for Mr. and Mrs. John Hay Whitney, Jansen, the renowned decorating firm in Paris, was installing the entire apartment on Fifth Avenue for Mr. and Mrs. William Paley.

Betsey Whitney was one of the three Cushing sisters, from Boston, who were all renowned for their beauty and style. Her first marriage to James Roosevelt, son of President Franklin Delano Roosevelt, ended in divorce. One of her two sisters, Minnie, was first married to Vincent Astor and then to the American artist, James Fosburgh. Her other sister, Barbara, known as Babe, was first married to the social blue-blood Stanley Mortimer. After they were divorced, she married William Paley, the founder and chairman of CBS. Babe was a much-loved client of Billy Baldwin.

One morning Betsey called and asked Sis and me to come for lunch at Greentree, the Whitneys's Long Island house. She said we needed to discuss an important, top-secret job that she did not want to talk about over the telephone. When we arrived, she told us that the guest wing of their house had to be redone, and quickly, because the newly married Princess Margaret and Lord Snowdon were coming for a visit. They wanted their time with the Whitneys to be quiet, with absolutely no publicity.

As Sis and I thought of appropriate things for the rooms, Betsey was not pleased with one of our ideas. She was terribly fond of the pairs of antique twin beds that were in the two guest rooms and did not want them replaced. I finally convinced her that the beds had to be removed when I said, "Betsey, can you imagine a member of the royal family sleeping on a single bed?" By having a closet removed, we were able to connect the two bedrooms. While we used certain English and Irish fabrics and appointments that we knew would be familiar to the royal couple, we also put in typically American things like patchwork quilts and small hooked rugs.

PRECEDING PAGES
*Sitting room for Mrs. John
Hay Whitney's plantation,
Greenwood, Thomasville, Georgia*

LEFT
*A corner of the guest room
of the Whitney house, Greentree,
in Manhasset, New York*

FOLLOWING PAGES
*Mrs. Whitney's bedroom
in Saratoga, New York*

*The John Hay Whitney indoor
swimming pool at Greentree*

Soon after the completion of our first work for the Whitneys, Sis and I journeyed to London for our annual spring buying trip for furniture and objects for our clients. We first made the rounds of the best shops, but never failed to visit favorite haunts that were not necessarily on the A-list. It was in one of these that the keen eye of Sister Parish spotted a small rectangular beaded pillow of Victorian vintage. Delicately worked in pastel colors, words on the pillow simply said Welcome Babe. *Sis immediately bought the pillow. I wondered at her choice and uttered my often "Why?" Sis's only reply was, "We shall see." The next week when we returned, an appointment had been made in our absence for Mrs. William Paley to come to our offices. There was, of course, great excitement and considerable wonder.*

When Babe Paley arrived mid-week, she was more charming and alluringly beautiful than one could imagine. After brief pleasantries, we learned that the purpose of the visit was to discuss the possibility of our working together to complete the totally unfinished drawing room in the Paley's Fifth Avenue apartment. Needless to say, we accepted her invitation to see the drawing room and to meet Mr. Paley.

Just as Mrs. Paley rose from her chair to be on her way, Sis, still seated, reached into her handbag on the floor beside her, and presented the beaded-work pillow that said Welcome Babe *to the glamorous Mrs. Paley. Great whoops of laughter broke out all around. Babe Paley thoroughly enjoyed the offering, and Sis was very pleased with herself.*

Our first visit to the Paleys's apartment was memorable. We entered the high-ceilinged room through double doors that were in line with the center of three tall windows, making up the opposite elevation, that looked out across Fifth Avenue to Central Park. The beautiful paneling that Jansen had installed in the spacious room, copied from a Paris eighteenth-century hôtel particulier that had long been a favorite of Bill Paley, was prime-coated with off-white paint. A fireplace was centered on one of the end walls but no chimneypiece had been installed. The floor of the room was exceptional, laid with old wood in the manner of parquet de Versailles. All in all, it was an excellent but simple canvas on which to work.

We were duly shown the inventory of furnishings to be incorporated in the overall design, including an attractive collection of very good chairs and tables, eighteenth-century French for the most part, and a tall red-lacquered ten-panel Oriental screen of great age and beauty. Most important of all was their collection of mid-twentieth-century paintings.

Before the meeting ended the subject of color was addressed, a suitable background color. Babe Paley preferred a light, warm ivory white—a neutral background—appropriate for the paneling; I agreed. Bill Paley then asked Sister for her opinion, and she threw us all a curve! Her idea of taxicab yellow seemed to pique Mr. Paley's imagination, leaving the rest of us somewhat at a loss, to put it mildly! But taxicab yellow it would be.

Never one to shy away from good, clear color, I worked with our team of expert painters to create a background of great spirit and beauty. Five different subtle shades of yellow were employed to produce the final effect. Taxicab yellow it was but with a soft, glowing luster.

The room had a freshness that proclaimed its own time and place—a ravishing mid-twentieth-century room. The furnishings established authority and the artwork gave enormous vitality. A perfect fit for the Paleys, people who expressed great style, quality and spirit in their daily lives.

We also did work for the Paleys at Kiluna Farm, their house in Manhasset, New York. When Bill Paley bought Four Fountains, the house on Long Island that had been owned by Eleanor and Archibald Brown, we were commissioned to do the interiors.

One of the many commissions that Hadley takes great pride in is the work he did for Mrs. Nelson Rockefeller after her husband died. Jean-Michel Frank, one of the designers Hadley most admires, had designed the living room for Governor Rockefeller and his first wife.

After Nelson Rockefeller died in 1982, Happy, as Mrs. Rockefeller is known, asked me to work with her on the details and furnishing of her new apartment. She had sold part of the apartment which included the original living room that was designed in 1937 by Jean-Michel Frank in collaboration with Christian Bérard, and the Giacometti brothers, Alberto and Diego. Photographs of the room, which was considered one of the most important interiors in America, had been published many times.

My first questions to Happy were about her plans for the Jean-Michel Frank furnishings and the ceiling designed by Jean Arp. When Happy said she had not given much thought to either, I convinced her that, above everything else, we must preserve these pieces and retain the integrity of the original design. While some things did not work with the new scheme, which was much lighter, most of the original furnishings were used. While the rooms were completely redone, the original look was saved.

In 1984 New York's mayor, Ed Koch, had Gracie Mansion, the official residence of the city's mayor, restored. Over the years the place had become run-down from use and needed a complete face-lift. I was asked to be on the decorating committee. Understanding that the house would continue to be used as the mayor's residence, my idea was to make the room both historically correct and suitable for everyday life. The antique paper I selected for the walls was printed by the Paris firm Zuber in the nineteenth century. In 2002, when Mayor Bloomberg ordered that Gracie Mansion be transformed into the "People's Museum" and made more accessible to city agencies for meetings and events, I wondered what would happen to my dining room. When Jamie Drake, the New York decorator who was in charge of the project, saw my original sketch for the room, he realized the chandelier I proposed was never hung, probably for budget reasons at the time. Jamie added a very fine period chandelier and left the room as I had designed it.

When it was announced that Vice President and Mrs. Albert Gore had asked Hadley to work on their home in Washington, D.C., there was little surprise. It is standard practice for elected officials and politicians to favor the talents of their constituents. Vice President Gore and Hadley are both sons of Tennessee. After Hadley completed his work, one reviewer said, "The Vice President's residence may have begun as down-home Tennessee but the final result is pure New York chic."

I was first introduced to Vice President Albert Gore by my Washington friends, Jim and Ann Free. When his second term in office began, Vice President and Mrs. Gore invited me to Washington to give them some advice on how best to use their furniture. The official residence of the vice president is a large house on the grounds of the Naval Observatory. Originally, it was the home of the superintendent of the observatory.

PAGES 146–151
*Vice President and Mrs.
Albert Gore's residence,
Washington, D.C.*

When I saw it, the house had been neglected for years and was in need of much repair. What began as an informal meeting to discuss furniture arrangement turned into a major project.

When I started with Sis, one of the first things I did was to help finish the work on the White House for the Kennedys. Seventeen years later, I was back in the political arena. The Gores were extraordinary clients and made my return to Washington a lot of fun. The job was a great success and received enthusiastic press coverage, which pleased us all.

Hadley expresses a genuine respect, if not fondness, for all of his clients and finds certain things in each job that make the work unusual. There is, however, one client that he remembers and talks about that has a unique place in his personal history. That person is Mrs. Vincent Astor.

It is probably safe to say that most present-day New Yorkers know the name Mrs. Vincent Astor or Brooke Astor, as she is fondly called. No woman, in this century or the last, has more securely held her place as

the quintessential figure in New York City's high society. In the nineteenth century this distinction was also held by an Astor, but stories about her formidable character lead one to believe that she, Mrs. William B. Astor, Jr. (née Caroline Webster Schermerhorn), was not in any way loved and admired like the present Mrs. Astor. Brooke Astor's place in the annals of New York City is of such importance that in Kenneth Jackson's *Encyclopedia of New York City*, she is given a separate entry from her late husband, Vincent. Jackson notes her work as a features editor at *House & Garden*, an author of two books, and her devoted oversight of the Vincent Astor Foundation. At the foundation, Mrs. Astor supervised the donation of nearly two hundred million dollars in grants that benefited the city's cultural and educational organizations and projects serving the poor and the disadvantaged. After one of her recent birthday celebrations, the *New York Times* referred to Mrs. Astor as the fairy godmother of New York City.

I shall never forget the first time I met Brooke Astor. I was working at McMillen. Mrs. Brown asked me to have lunch with her at the River Club, a very swanky establishment at the end of East Fifty-second Street. Our firm was doing some work for the club at the time. Mrs. Astor joined us. I think that she was on the club's house decoration committee. She was extremely attractive, beautifully dressed in a simple summer linen outfit. At the time, she was an editor at House & Garden. *She had just come from seeing some rooms that Cecil Beaton had decorated at the St. Regis Hotel. Beaton had done the rooms in a black-and-white print wallpaper and matching fabric—a smart design from a new company called The Pippin Papers. He had used the pattern everywhere, "Even the lampshades!" Brooke said. She was bubbling with excitement—so full of life, so enthusiastic, so vivacious. I was enchanted and thought, "What a woman!"*

When I joined Sis, she had been doing work for the Astors for years. She had decorated the interiors of their New York City apartment and Ferncliff, their house in Rhinebeck, New York. Because the house contained an indoor tennis court and swimming pool, Vincent called it The Playhouse. This was the house where Van Truex designed the carpet for the library, a spotted creation to accommodate Vincent Astor's miniature ponies, which were allowed to roam freely in the room. After Vincent's death, Brooke gave Ferncliff to an order of Roman Catholic nuns. Sis and I both worked on her new house, Holly Hill, in Briarcliff Manor, New York.

One of the most challenging and exciting projects that Sis and I worked on together for Brooke Astor began over tea in her apartment. After meeting us at the door, Brooke immediately led us into a small anteroom off the main hall and we went down a beautifully detailed, gracefully curving stairway to the apartment below. The illustrious architect Page Cross had recently designed and supervised the installation of the stairway, which opened onto an impressive long, wide gallery. Sis and I were both curious about what was to happen next. We knew that the apartment was the home of Brooke's mother, Mrs. Russell, who had recently died. We had no further clue.

Over tea in the spacious drawing room that was furnished with an assembly of some very good eighteenth-century French furniture, mostly chairs, and an enormous grand piano, curiosity won the day and Sis asked, "Tell me, Brooke, what do you plan to do with this?"

Without hesitation and in her winning, jovial manner, her reply was simply, "Oh Sister, this is where I plan to give away Vincent's money!"

Knowing that Brooke was the head of the Vincent Astor Foundation, the philanthropic organization of her late husband, her answer came as no surprise. One could easily imagine reception rooms, boardrooms, and offices. That was not Brooke's plan. The room that we were sitting in was to become a more up-to-date drawing room that would be suitable for entertaining and musicals. A guest bedroom was to be outfitted employing a lively color scheme. There also was to be an adjacent small sitting room. Sis and I were in total accord with Brooke's plans. She then told us that in just a few days, she would be leaving for Europe where she would spend the next month visiting friends. Then came the cruncher!

She wanted us to do all of the work in one month and have the rooms completed when she returned. If we had seen television shows like we see today—where entire houses are made over in ten days—we would not have given the schedule a thought. To be honest, we were not given a crushing deadline, but expectations were high. We immediately made plans, established a clear point of view, and rounded up our assistants, artists, and artisans. An expert team was ready for action.

A Louis XV rouge royal-marble mantel, centered on one long wall of the large, high-ceilinged room, was flanked on either side by a pair of doors. The opposite wall consisted of a parade of three evenly spaced, tall windows. One end wall had tall bookshelves set into paneling; the other end was the backdrop for the dark, gleaming concert grand piano.

The wooden floor, a large-scale herringbone pattern of different widths, was stained in alternating bands of dark and light. We had a Tree of Life design, taken from an antique fragment of crewelwork, screen printed a dark creosote color on fine, natural linen. This fabric would be used for curtains at the three tall windows. Attached to small gilded poles, set at the top of the window molding, the curtains were designed to hang straight and barely skim the floor. Our upholstery shop was busy putting new fabrics—cottons, linens, and raw silk, all in neutral shades—on the old furniture frames. A crew of painters was busy creating the background. The preparation seemed endless. The month would soon be up.

The flat-paneled walls were painted in shades ranging from parchment and ivory to muted golds and tobacco. The ancient technique that was used is known as Italian marbling. Drawing inspiration from the patterns of exotic marble, the highly decorative technique is not intended to fool the eye. Wood paneling that has been subjected to this primitive process has great style and allure. The aggressive scale of the marbling technique and the light values of the paint colors resulted in a glowing play of light and shadow.

The tapestry of books in the end wall added color and warmth to a rather stylistic scheme as did other objects of note. A large down sofa,

*Mrs. Vincent Astor's
Park Avenue dining room*

covered in a parchment-colored striped fabric, held its own beneath the books. The sense of luxe was completed by a pair of large square down pillows covered in a black/brown dull satin fabric that added luster and a contrasting texture to the scene. The last gaping spaces in the room—between the tall windows—were attended to when Sis turned up with a pair of incredibly beautiful consoles, from India, made of light wood inlaid with mother-of-pearl. This was done without any measurements, as was Sis's manner. Only possible with her magic eye!

The guest room came into focus along the way, bypassing any thought of a debutante's lair. A sophisticated scheme was created, which required making a copy of a painted canopy twin bed that Brooke had used when she was a young girl. The room was colorful and comfortable, a haven for travel-weary guests.

The sitting room was another story. The room was comparatively small. The two north windows produced a cool even light. Pale-colored fabrics in various textures and small patterns were used to cover the furniture and make the simple curtains. The floor was carpeted in natural-colored straw matting. To add luster and bring animation to the space the walls were finished in a rich deep red, high-gloss paint.

Above the snuff-colored linen damask sofa, we hung a very decorative nineteenth-century painting of dogs—black whippets, to be exact—portrayed in a mannerism pose. The painting was one that Sis and I had bought on our most recent trip to London. Quite at the last minute, we decided to use it for this prominent place of honor. Actually, it didn't seem to be Brooke's "thing" but the month was coming to an end.

All in all, the results were good and it was a great adventure "playing house" with Brooke when she returned. Her keen eye darted about the finished rooms and only occasionally was she prompted to slightly reposition a small chair or move an object.

The surprising thing was that she zeroed in on the stylish black hounds to such an extent that within days she was on the search for more paintings of dogs. This time, to put on the bare wall of the tall curving stairway in her country house Holly Hill in Briarcliff Manor. When the word got out that Mrs. Vincent Astor was collecting dog paintings, every antiques and picture dealer both here and abroad suddenly had more dogs for sale than one could imagine! It was a new venture for her and one that proved to be exceptional.

157

*Mrs. Vincent Astor's bedroom
in New York City*

Today, the tall, curved wall in the stair hall is literally paved with a collection of charming, and sometimes rare, examples of canine portraiture. Her collection includes works by artists who created likenesses of her own dogs and those of her friends' dogs.

What a lady!

When Brooke asked me to decorate her dining room in New York, she said the eighteenth-century French wall panels had to remain. The panels were pastoral scenes done in sepia and romantic pale pinks. Brooke made up her mind that the room should also be pink. It took a lot of convincing to get her to let me paint the walls a deep rich peacock blue, a minor color that was also in the panels and thus put the panels in high relief. When she said she wanted the curtains to look like ball gowns, I designed them in peacock blue and pink silk taffeta, in the style of belle epoque haute-couture dresses. Everything in the room was from Brooke's collection of eighteenth-century French furniture.

While Mrs. Astor's French furniture and traditional design sense is evident in Hadley's stories, she also had strong interests in things that are contemporary. This is apparent in Hadley's description of the work he did on her bedroom and her desire to have the freshness of hand-blocked cotton fabrics on eighteenth-century antiques.

After Brooke first saw the lively color palette of Alan Campbell, the batik artist who did a lot of work for us, she was madly enthusiastic about his work. I was summoned to create a new environment for her New York bedroom using Alan's fabrics. The room was at the end of a long hallway. The entrance was directly opposite an imposing, classically-shaped Louis XVI bed with high head- and footboards and a fabric canopy. The windows that flanked the bed were set well apart, giving more than ample space at the bedside. Centered on the shorter wall to the right, was a Louis XVI marble chimneypiece. Hanging over the fireplace was a contemporary painting in arresting shades of pink, gold, and pale blue. The opposite elevation was comprised of a pair of windows that were separated by considerable wall space.

Brooke Astor's enthusiasm for every detail pertaining to the furnishing and decorating of her rooms is charmingly effective. No one can equal her gaiety of spirit, her joyous laughter, and her keen wit. Like so

many people, Brooke first began thinking of color but it took only a moment to tune her interest to my insistence of first creating a plan of structure and space.

My first proposal was to reposition the bed, placing it between the two windows on the short wall, which would free the center of the room for a more congenial arrangement of furniture. On the wall where the bed had been, I placed a beautiful, rather large light-wood desk and chairs. Over the desk I hung the painting that had originally held center stage over the fireplace. Here it was the focal point when viewing the room from the long hallway. To reflect light and add sparkle to the room, a large gilt-framed oval mirror was now over the mantel. As all of the changes were taking place, a color scheme of soft, fresh spring green and ivory was developed, using Alan Campbell's fabrics.

For the walls and straight hanging curtains I chose a fabric with an overall pattern in shades of green. The fabric for the walls was paper-backed and applied like wallpaper. This is often done to simplify back-grounds. All of the wood trim in the room was painted a soft white and the scheme was anchored by a carpet that was a few shades darker. The same fabric that covered the walls was used to cover a charming small Louis XV slipper chair. The frame of the chair had its original eighteenth-century white paint.

In the far corner of the room, angled between the window and the fireplace, a large, luxurious upholstered chaise longue, covered in an off-white French matelassé *fabric, formed the axis of a comfortable seating group. Next to the chaise was a low rectangular Lucite table stacked with books and magazines.*

160

Sketch for Mr. and Mrs. Garrick Stephenson

Needless to say, attention had to be focused on the cumbersome Louis XVI bed. Even in its original position, the high footboard blocked any possible view. Perhaps this was just as well. If by chance the door had been open, the only view from the bed would have been the long hallway. Now placed between the windows, with the footboard removed, the bed faced the fireplace. Billowing Swiss muslin fell from a crown above the headboard. The muslin was attached at four corners before it cascaded to the floor. On one side of the bed, a large glass-topped table, with a Lucite base, held a collection of personal photographs, flowers, and a few decorative objects. On the other side, affording convenience and comfort, was a white-lacquered rectangular table with a clear surface top, a long single drawer, and a shelf below.

In the daytime, warm light from the near windows, on the long wall, envelops the bed and Brooke can see blue skies and floating clouds; at night she can count the stars. The final results were amazingly soft and feminine. It was a room of beautiful color and light that reflected a very personal attitude—a point of view that is at once classical and well grounded, but with a cutting edge of the moment. It is the point of view of a woman, Mrs. Vincent Astor, who is loath to follow the dictates of fashion but in no way shies away from an adventure.

The most important job that Hadley ever did for Mrs. Astor is undoubtedly the library in her Park Avenue apartment. Libraries have been important to the Astor family since John Jacob Astor gave a bequest of four hundred thousand dollars to establish the first public library in New York City in

1849. When Vincent Astor died he had an extraordinarily valuable and beautiful collection of books that Brooke held in storage. From time to time she mentioned to Hadley that she worried about the safekeeping of the books.

I was working at the office one morning when Brooke phoned and said, "Albert, can you come over for tea this afternoon? It will just be the two of us." I accepted knowing that something was up. Tea for two means that something confidential will be discussed.

At four o'clock I rang her bell. I was ushered into a room that was called the library. Like many very expensive Park Avenue apartments in buildings built in the twenties and thirties, the walls of the room were covered with fake Louis XV paneling. It was not, by any stretch of the imagination, real French boiserie. It was stained a soft walnut color and here and there were some small recessed cabinets with doors that had typical chicken-wire panels. It certainly wasn't a library.

After tea was brought in and we were alone, Brooke started to confess why I had been called over. "Albert, I have something to tell you. Something that I know is going to make Sister furious." Sis had recently refurbished the room using Brunschwig & Fils "Portuguesa" on the sofa and two Odom chairs. It was all very appropriate and beautiful. I knew Brooke was leading to something that she considered serious and delicate. I assured her she had my strictest confidence.

"Well," she continued, "do you know who I mean by Geoffrey Bennison?"

Of course I did. At the time Geoffrey had an antiques shop in London that Sis and I always visited when we were in England. He had great style

PRECEDING PAGES
*The Gustavo Cisneros house,
Caracas, Venezuela*

RIGHT
*Dining room designed for
Mr. and Mrs. John Radziwill*

PAGES 172–175
*Penthouse designed for Mr. and
Mrs. Edward O'Herron, Charlotte,
North Carolina*

and rather romantic taste. He accepted decorating commissions from only a privileged few. In a somewhat apologetic tone Brooke continued. "Geoffrey is in town and I have asked him to decorate the library, this room. I know this is going to upset Sis and I need your help. Tell me what to say to her and tell me that you will help her to understand."

I was direct in confirming her fear that Sis would be upset. Sis considered the Astor properties her territory and hers alone. I knew that she would be angry if Brooke called in another decorator. At the same time I told Brooke that Sis would get over it. "Brooke, it is your apartment. You can have whomever you wish to work for you." To help calm Brooke's nervousness, and out of my own curiosity, I asked if Bennison had given her any idea of what he had in mind for the room. Had he presented any plans? This got Brooke very excited and she said that in fact she had both some sketches he had done and samples of the fabrics that he wanted to use. She showed it all to me. My response was to say that the renderings of the draperies were magnificent, worthy of a museum. After I had seen the drawings and a few of the proposed fabric samples, she said with her characteristic enthusiasm, "Now what do you think? What do you really think?"

"Do you really want to know what I think?"

"Yes, please continue."

"Well first of all Brooke, this room is not about fabrics; it is about books. If you say it is a library, it should be a library. And on top of that, the paneling in this room is the only thing in your life that is fake. Get rid of it. For years you have talked about Vincent's books. This is your chance to use them. Build the room around the books. Make it a twentieth-century room. Make the room the Astor Library."

I could tell immediately that she liked the idea and insisted that I tell her more.

"What do you mean?" she said. "What would you do?"

Of course I hadn't a clue. I was just talking but I said, while it should be classical in spirit, it must also be a room to live in. Not knowing what was structurally possible, I said that we would replace the walls with floor-to-ceiling bookcases. When she asked me about color, I was again without a clue but from somewhere came "red lacquer and brass." I did not hesitate to tell her that it would mean the total dismantling of the room and a complete architectural restructuring.

"Oh, Albert, I love the idea. Show me what you mean."

Back to the office I went. When I returned just before six, Sis wanted to know where I had been. I told her that Brooke had invited me for tea and went on to tell her what had happened. Her reaction was just as I told Brooke it would be—she was furious. After Brooke accepted my final plans and the work began, Sis was very supportive but she could be negative as the work went on, saying things like, "I had lunch with Brooke and she is getting very upset that the work on the library is taking so long." I would then find some reason to call Brooke and make sure she was not upset. Never once did she complain. Her only comment, which was consistent, was "It is going to be so beautiful when it is finished." Ten coats of oxblood-red paint were applied to get the right glaze. When the job was finished, it was very successful. Of all the rooms that I have ever done, Brooke Astor's library remains my favorite. Today, whenever we are in the room, Brooke never fails to say, "Albert, Vincent would be so pleased."

The Astor Library went on to become one of the iconic rooms in American interior design. During the tenure of the last six presidents of the United States, Mrs. Astor has entertained each of them in this room. Here she has received numerous heads of state, ambassadors, prelates, and foreign aristocrats. Pictures of the room have been published in magazines and journals throughout the world. It is undoubtedly the most photographed room in the history of American interior decorating. With all of the luster and note the library has gained since Hadley finished working his design genius, the library remains an intimate setting for Mrs. Astor's private life. It is the place where she sits alone to read or have tea with friends. It is the room where a folding table is often placed before the fire on an autumn day. Covered with a white cut-work, Swiss embroidery cotton cloth reaching the floor, the table is set by maids dressed in pink uniforms with white aprons. Here Brooke has intimate lunches with one or two, three at the most, of her close friends. There beneath her Childe Hassam painting, *Flags Flying on Fifth Avenue*, she continues a fast-fading tradition—lunch served by one's personal uniformed staff in one's own home. Hadley had succeeded in what he set out to do—beyond a room for books, he had made a space beautiful for a woman who lives alone, a room that can be used for entertaining dignitaries or her closest friends. Hadley created a masterpiece.

PAGES 180–185
*Apartment designed for Mr. Vincent Friia,
San Francisco*

Mr. and Mrs. Thornton Wilson's
Manhattan dining room

RIGHT
The New York drawing room
of Mrs. Enid Haupt

FACING PAGE
*Vintage print of a bachelor's apart-
ment, Chicago. Curtain fabric
designed by D. D. and Leslie Tillet*

ABOVE
Batik designs by Alan Campbell

FOLLOWING PAGES
*The Far Hills, New Jersey,
library designed for Mr. and
Mrs. Thornton Wilson*

189

PRECEDING PAGES
Living room designed for Mr. and Mrs. Carter Burden, River House, New York City

Dining room and living room designed for Renée Meyers, Manhattan

*Vintage prints of a
New York City bedroom*

FOLLOWING PAGES
*Parish-Hadley, Inc., reception room
in the Fuller Building, Madison
Avenue and Fifty-seventh Street,
New York City.*

A Decorator
Is Never Alone

PRECEDING PAGES
Happy

Decorators must have craftsmen who produce their work. For some projects they need construction workers, carpenters, plumbers, and electricians to fabricate their plans. Decorators also need painters, wallpaper hangers, upholsterers, curtain makers, and people who specialize in custom lighting, furniture, and finishing details such as decorative wall finishes. Knowing that excellent workmanship is a prerequisite in every one of their commissions, good decorators must seek workers who are dependable and the best in their trade.

Interior designers also need vendors who supply them with fabrics, wall coverings, rugs, and decorative objects. They must know the home furnishings and antiques markets and regularly search for new, exciting, and beautiful goods that are appropriate for their clients. When all of these many facets of interior decorating come together, beautiful rooms are produced. During the many years that Albert Hadley has been in the decorating business, his suppliers have served him well and, like his clients, many of them are his best friends.

When I think about the work that I have done over the years, I know that none of it could have been possible without the help of the artisans and craftsmen that I have worked with. While I have had the privilege of knowing many of these men and women personally, no one stands out in my mind like Alan Campbell.

Alan was originally from North Carolina. After graduating from Princeton, he worked in the Foreign Service and traveled all over the world. At some point, I don't know exactly when, Alan came to New York and was hired by the John D. Rockefeller III Fund. In some way, he was involved in their Asian art collection. One evening when he came with a mutual friend to my new apartment, he brought me a small piece of batik, about four inches square, he had designed. It was a charming picture of a purple dog on an orange background. Allen said that making batik prints was his new hobby. It so happened that I was working on a commission that was being done in black, tan, and brown. I suggested to Alan that he design some twenty-inch-square batik prints that I could use for accent pillows.

It was not long after our first meeting that Alan came to our offices with some very exciting batik prints, done in geometric, somewhat

African patterns, in colors that I could use for my black, tan, and brown scheme. They were absolutely fabulous and I immediately asked him to do more. When Sis saw his batiks, she wanted to know where they came from and who did them. When I told her that my friend Alan Campbell was the batik artist, she took several of the pieces—just walked out with them—and used them in a scheme that she was working on. Like me, Sis was very excited about Alan's work and wanted to meet him.

The following Sunday evening, Alan came to Sis's open house. It was the first of many visits. At one of her parties, he met the fashion designer Halston. After seeing Alan's work, Halston commissioned him to do some batiks for his new and very chic caftans. Suddenly Alan Campbell had so much work making batiks that he quit his job with the Rockefeller Fund and opened his business, Alan Campbell Fabrics and Wallpapers, which was a huge success. He remained a very dear friend.

Today the custom wallpapers and fabrics that I design are produced by the Zina Studios in Mount Vernon, New York. Count and Countess Nicholas Bobrinskoy, the owners and designers at Zina, specialize in museum-quality work. The two of them have absolute control over everything that is produced in their studio and their work is magnificent. Recently I had a gentleman, a true old-world artisan, come out of retirement to paint the walls of a dining room to resemble an antique Chinese wallpaper. It is this kind of special detail that sets a room apart. It is also important for decorators to know excellent cabinetmakers, furniture restorers, and artists who produce special finishes such as lacquer, shagreen, tortoise shell, and faux marble.

Since I've been in the decorating business in New York City for fifty years, I am now working with the children and grandchildren of craftsmen I started with. Certainly this is true of the upholstery firms that I use. When I started at McMillen, it was a great privilege and learning experience to work with the master upholsterer Guido de Angelis, who did all of Mrs. Brown's work. When I started with Sis, her upholstery was done by A. Schneller and Sons. The Schnellers worked with all the old-guard decorators, going back to Elsie de Wolfe and Bill Pahlmann. Today, I continue to work with the de Angelis family and the Schnellers. Having done business with the original Mr. Schneller, today I deal with his

Betsy

grandson Jon and his wife Pam. Both firms, Schneller and de Angelis, are more than upholsterers, they are true artists with remarkable taste. Everything they do is hands-on and top quality.

If you are as picky as I am, it is necessary to have someone who understands what you want. Unless it's done right, it never looks right. If an arm gets too much padding or gets too heavy, then you lose the whole thing. It is the small measurements that make the big differences in suitable furniture. Most of my clients expect fine workmanship and are willing to pay for it.

Preferring to do residential work, Parish-Hadley Inc. took on very few corporate or commercial jobs. They did the offices for Tommy Mottola at Sony, the lobby and reception area of Columbia Artists Management, Inc., and both the corporate offices and Madison Avenue boutique for Judith Leiber. The firm decorated the partners' dining room and the executive dining room in both the William Street and Water Street offices of Lehman Brothers Kuhn Loeb. They also decorated the executive offices, executive dining rooms, the boardroom, and client meeting rooms for The Bank of New York. In Sarasota and Miami, they designed the main banking floor, executive office, and boardroom for the Northern Trust Company. When the Ritz-Carlton Hotel opened on Central Park South in

Eugénie

New York City, they designed the entire hotel, including the lobby, dining rooms, guest rooms, and suites. Parish-Hadley also designed the Jockey Club in the Ritz-Carlton in Washington, D.C. For Tiffany & Co. Parish-Hadley designed the complete interior of their store in Dallas. Before Condé Nast moved to Times Square they designed their executive offices, conference rooms, and reception areas. In 1993 the firm produced the Parish-Hadley furniture collection for Baker, Knapp & Tubbs. They also designed a line of fabrics for Lee Jofa. In 2000, Hadley did the Albert Hadley Collection of fabrics and wallpapers for Hinson & Co. He also has his own collection of tables, chairs, lamps, and lighting fixtures that are custom-made for his work.

Because he started his work with Mrs. Parish on New Year's Day, Hadley thinks nothing of working holidays, weekends, and late nights, and being up before dawn to get started on a job. "Getting it right" is one of his favorite expressions. "Doing whatever is necessary to get the job done" is another.

I often go to the workrooms on Saturday, when everyone is away for the weekend, and quietly check on the progress of my orders. Whenever I commission custom upholstery, I do the original sketches and turn them over to professionals who work out the details.

Now there is a new generation coming along that doesn't want a custom-made sofa that will last for fifty or a hundred years. They want something that they can buy immediately without spending a lot of money. Recently I did a project in Washington, D.C., and everything we used came out of Crate and Barrel or Pottery Barn. Many of the things made in today's mass market are well designed and well constructed. In some ways, the things are the dream of the Bauhaus come true—quality home furnishings for the masses.

Since his time on the faculty at Parsons School of Design, Hadley has been the proverbial teacher. One of his assistants said, "Whenever he is reviewing our work or going over a job with us, he is always teaching, guiding." Over the years he has developed his own mantras and unalterable maxims.

When a job requires special lighting, we always call in an expert. Design is defined by light and shade and appropriate lighting is enormously important. With the many new methods of illumination, a decorator has to be careful to not overdo lighting. This is an easy trap for a designer to fall into—going too far in dramatizing interiors. Dramatic lighting will photograph well, but that doesn't always make for comfortable living and can look commercial. When we light a room our objective is to get rid of gloom, to have enough light to feel happy.

When I work with painters, I mix the colors that I use. After I have mixed the right color, the painters then mix the quantities that are needed for the job. Color has to do with light and the correct color can only be mixed on the job, in the space where it will be used.

While I enjoy antiques, I'm not interested so much in the museum quality of an object as I am in its integrity and aesthetic dynamics. To me it is much more interesting to have things that have a quirky personality. I am not interested in furniture made by particular names or things that are distinguished by an unusual provenance. Almost everything I own has some personal meaning, like the black satin hat marker that my grandmother embroidered for my grandfather before their wedding. I have a small rock on which my mother painted a likeness of my house, called Fort William, in Pocantico, New York. All of my furnishings are things that I have had for a long time—things from my family or that I've collected. My apartment and my house in Southport [Connecticut] are sort of like scrapbooks of my past.

The one thing I never get involved with is selecting art or pictures for a client. This is a very personal thing. If the clients have pictures, I will hang them. When they do not own pictures I leave the walls blank. Personally, I like prints and black-and-white photographs. In my house in Southport I have a collection of cat photographs by the late Fernando Bengoechea. One of his photographs that I have in my apartment is of two eggs that appear to be floating. Of course my favorite paintings, which are actually ink-wash drawings, are by Van Day Truex. A lot of my own sketches are in my office and from time to time I hang one or two of my own collages.

While I like the things that I own, I don't have anything that I could not live without. I am constantly moving things around, passing them on to friends—a sort of sharing—and when it is appropriate, using things I own in decorating schemes. When I use something that I have owned for many years in a project for a client, I don't think of it as getting rid of something. For me, it is like keeping things in the family.

My one piece of furniture that I am especially fond of is an early twentieth-century German pyramidal bookcase of black lacquer made to commemorate the athletes of the 1936 Olympics. I found it over forty years ago in a Third Avenue secondhand furniture store. My Italian biennale lamp that Van Truex introduced to America in 1949 is another thing that holds special memories for me. For some reason, over the years, these things have stayed with me but I could live without them.

Seashells have always been my one indulgence. I suppose you might say I am a collector. We're all collectors by nature. But if you're talking about an orderly life, there has to be a stop sign somewhere. Building a collection requires a strong constitution and the ability to resist.

Two of the things in my apartment that bring back happy memories are my portrait of Elsie de Wolfe and my Diana Vreeland V. After I bought the portrait, I had Elsie de Wolfe look at it, and she said, "I didn't sit for that. It was done for a newspaper, and the damned fool, flipping through clippings, got Anne Morgan's head on my body. But I'll tell you that it's a portrait of me and that will make it much more interesting and much more valuable." My V is a gouache painting by Alexander Liberman. It came from the Vreeland estate sale held at Sotheby's. I was sick at the time of the sale and someone called from my office and said, "If you were going to the sale, what thing of Diana Vreeland's would you rather have than anything else?" And I said, I didn't really want anything, but the thing I've always liked a lot was the V. The people in my office got together and bid on it, and they gave it to me as a present.

I refuse to let material things possess me. Holding on to things is not important to me. When I decorated my apartment and my house in Connecticut my intent was to be able to live more simply. If I achieve this, I know I have succeeded. Finally that is what I really care about—simplicity. There is no point in cluttering up your life with things that are not really meaningful. Over the years, in every place I've lived, I've set up what I call the "secret closet," where I store things that are no longer relevant to my life. I get excited about new ideas and new projects. A friend said to me not long ago that a rearview mirror is intended for a careful backward glance but the focus must be on the road ahead. Things that happen today are already dated. I think about the future. I learned this from Van Truex. This all brings up another matter, taste.

Taste can be a great stumbling block. A decorator must understand that taste is not a standard but the power to discern, to concentrate. Taste is an appreciation of order and a sure knowledge of what constitutes fitness. These concepts can be learned through education, travel, experience, and living. In learning these principles, the person will come to understand that a room—any room—is simply an enclosure of space

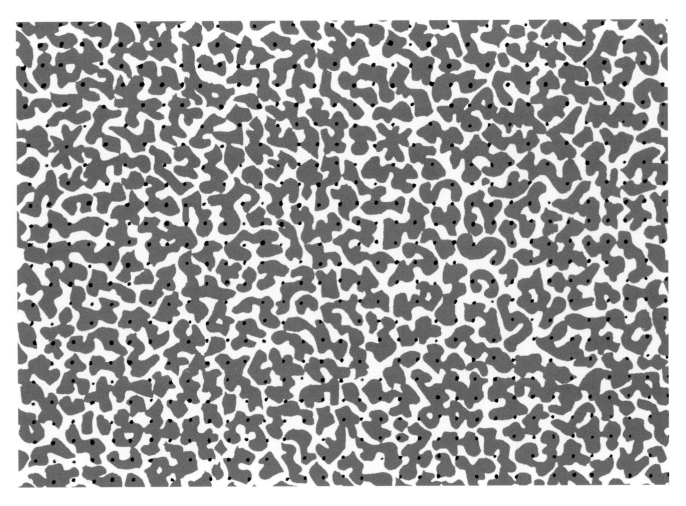

Jigsaw

and time for a specific purpose. The challenge is to know what is suitable in this defined space.

Flair is another thing. Flair is a primitive kind of style. It is innate and cannot be taught. It can be polished and refined. When a person has flair, a grounding in the principles of design, and self-discipline, that person has the potential of being an outstanding designer. The essence of interior design will always be about people and how they live. It is about the realities of what makes for an attractive, civilized, meaningful environment, not about fashion or what's in or what's out. This is not an easy job. A decorator, no matter how talented, can't always get the desired results because sometimes there is resistance or maybe a lack of understanding on the part of the client. I think it is the decorator's job to work as a guide, to bring out the best qualities and the best attitudes.

To create an interior, the designer must develop an overall concept and stick to it. He must be able to clarify his intent keeping ever in mind that decorating is not a look, it's a point of view. Once the theme is defined, everything that is added must amplify the original scheme; anything that does not must be subtracted. To do this the designer must be able to see—make a concentrated effort to absorb the essence of the project. Seeing is a very difficult thing to do. Most people "look" at a lot of things but never "see" anything. Looking is emotional; seeing is an intellectual process.

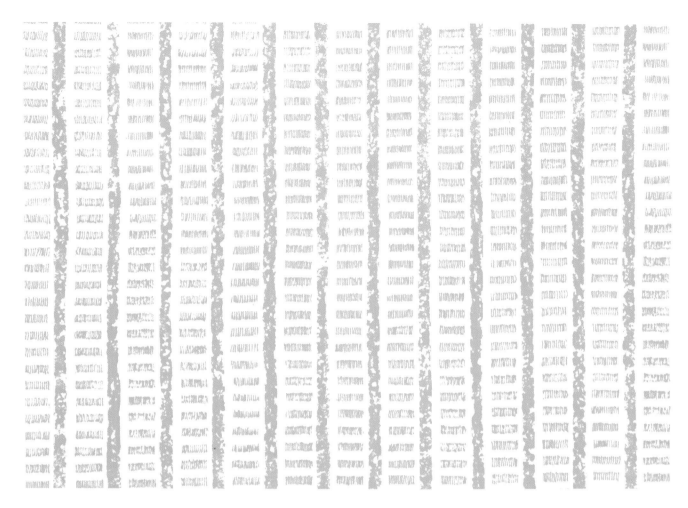

After the design is firmly fixed, the decoration is added. Decorating is the final enhancement. When Van Truex defined the difference between designing and decorating, he used the analogy of preparing a roast of beef. Design, he said, is the preparation and cooking; decorating is the final seasoning, the savoring.

Recalling the many honors and awards he has received and acknowledging the recognition that has come to him, Hadley says:

Through the years, the home furnishings editors at the New York Times *and the* New York Times Sunday Magazine, *there have been many, have been fantastic about publishing my work. I am especially grateful that Pilar Viladas and Billy Norwich, who are at the* Times *now, continue to write articles about what I am doing. All of the editors of the leading decorating magazines—Lou Gropp and Marian McEvoy who were at* House Beautiful, *and now Mark Mayfield; Anna Wintour, Babs Simpson, Mary Jane Pool, Nancy Novogrod, and Nancy Richardson who were at* House & Garden, *and now Dominique Browning; Lisa Newsom at* Veranda; *Margaret Russell at* Elle Decor; *and Paige Rense at* Architectural Digest— *have given me fabulous feature stories. Even the smaller regional magazines like* Westport *and* New Jersey Living *regularly report on my work. All of this is a very humbling experience.*

Albert Hadley, Inc.

In August 1994, after a lingering illness in New York City, Mrs. Parish was taken by hospital plane to Islesboro, Maine. On September 8, 1994, she died in her beloved house in Dark Harbor. A week later, her family and friends gathered on the island for her burial.

At the same time that Hadley struggled with the loss of his partner, he received notice that the building where the Parish-Hadley offices were located was being turned into cooperative apartments. After ten years at the 305 East Sixty-third Street location, the offices of Parish-Hadley, Inc. were moved to the Fuller Building at Fifty-seventh Street and Madison Avenue.

The design and decoration of the new offices was an in-house project. One designer who helped with the new space said, "It's Albert Hadley amplified; everything he knows is funneled into this one place. It appears to be simple, but to get the Hadley look requires years of refining."

Alone at the helm, Hadley had firm concepts of a new, bright look. When the offices were featured in *House Beautiful* he said, "Not everyone is enthusiastic about the changes I've made, but I'm not a sentimentalist. It's never hard for me to pull up. Our fresh point of view reflects a definite swing of the pendulum toward the young. If Sis were here, she would have put her two cents in—and would not have made the move easy—but finally, even with all of her traditional values, she would have been supportive of what we've done. Sis, don't forget, was a very modern woman."

Five years later, in 1999, Hadley was ready for a change. He closed the thirty-three-year-old firm of Parish-Hadley, Inc. Then seventy-nine, he was on the brink of a new adventure. The *New York Times* article that announced the closing of the firm was filled with praise for Hadley and his work. It referred to him as the "*éminence grise* of American design" and listed many of his most important clients and commissions. His two favorite idioms, "never more, never less" and, the one that he learned from the late Diana Vreeland, "give 'em what they never knew they wanted" were both included. Perhaps assuming that Hadley was retiring, the *Times* story was titled "Albert Hadley Draws the Shades" and the writer said his "edge will be missed," which gave an ominous note of finality.

Hadley had no intention of quitting or retiring when he closed Parish-Hadley, Inc. In the article he even said, "I'm not sure quite what I'm going to do, but I can't wait to do it." He later added, "It was the beginning of a new century. It was time to get on with things." The best of Albert Hadley was yet to come.

When Hadley was asked about his future plans, he talked about getting back to hands-on designing and having more direct contact with his clients. These things had been turned over to assistants as the business of Parish-Hadley, Inc. had grown. Hadley said he wanted time for his sketching and looked forward to working on his collages. In "Giants of Design," an article in *House Beautiful* in June 2000, when talking about his future plans, Hadley said, "The people who want me to work for them depend on me, and I've reached the point where I feel I might as well be in control. I have not been in control for the last twenty years. Sis and I employed and encouraged young designers to work intimately with clients who sought the firm's services. My role became more editorial. I always had the last word, but it was not like running a job from beginning to end, which I came to miss. It was a question of doing things duet rather than solo. I'm not sure how good I am at solo, but I'll try to sing as loudly as I can."

Sketch for a Kips Bay show house

His first stop, after closing Parish-Hadley Inc. was at 136 East Fifty-seventh Street. Pamela Banker, one of his former decorators, had her offices in the building and offered him a small space until he found a suitable location. When Hadley came to New York, as student in 1947, the offices and some of the classrooms of Parsons were at 136 East Fifty-seventh Street. When he moved into Pamela's office, he exclaimed, "I'm right back where I started!"

Nothing could have been farther from the truth. He most certainly was not the young man who struggled to pay his rent and turned down a scholarship in Paris because he didn't have the money to pay for his expenses. During the fifty years since he first came to New York, Hadley had been on an incredible journey. He began his career at the most prestigious decorating firm in America, McMillen, Inc. Following his years at

*Vintage print of Hadley's first
Kips Bay show house, 1974*

RIGHT
*Bathroom for Kips Bay show house,
1989*

McMillen, Hadley and his partner, Mrs. Henry Parish II, built Parish-Hadley, Inc. into a decorating firm that was second to none. Their clients included the president and the vice president of the United States, ambassadors, captains of industry, and America's most socially elite families. Parish-Hadley, Inc. was featured more times than any other firm or single decorator in the annual Kips Bay Show House in New York City. In 1970, Hadley and Mrs. Parish were among the select interior designers chosen to decorate for the Metropolitan Museum of Arts Centennial Anniversary celebration. The event was perhaps the biggest party ever given in New York City. Hadley and Mrs. Parish are the only interior designers whose work is in the permanent collection and archives of the Cooper-Hewitt, National Design Museum of the Smithsonian Institution.

Through his charm and subtle sophistication, Hadley has gathered unto himself a vast number of friends and fans from the upper crust of American society and the inner sanctums of business and politics. He also

Twenty-fifth anniversary
Kips Bay show house, 1997

Kips Bay show house, 2001
"Homage to Van Day Truex"

has a following of young friends and acolytes who relish his company. The list of citations he has received is extraordinary. The top honor in his profession came to him in 1986 when he was inducted into the Interior Design Hall of Fame. In 1992 he was made a Fellow of the American Society of Interior Designers, the organization's highest honor, and awarded an honorary doctorate degree from his alma mater, Parsons School of Design. Eight years later, in 2000, the New York School of Interior Design established the Albert Hadley Scholarship and conferred on him the degree of Doctor of Fine Arts.

On a personal note, Hadley has prospered in the fifty years that he has lived in New York City. He owns an apartment on the Upper East Side, just off of Fifth Avenue. In the early days of his partnership with Mrs. Parish he bought a summer place in Islesboro, Maine, where he spent his summer weekends. When he sold his Maine house, Hadley bought a weekend house that belonged to the Rockefeller family, near their estate, Kykuit, on the Hudson River. After ten years, he was weary of the isolation in Tarrytown and the "hopeless upkeep" of the large garden.

PRECEDING PAGES
Show house, Southampton,
New York

PAGES 222–227
Hadley's New York City
apartment

German bookcase in Hadley's
living room. Designed in 1936
to celebrate the Olympics held
in Berlin. Drawing on facing page
by Van Day Truex.

While taking a drive with his mother and his sister, Betsy, in Connecticut, Hadley spotted a small Italianate-Victorian cottage in the village of Southport. Remembering the first time that he saw the house, he said, "The house was waiting for me. It was the house I wanted." Originally, the little house had been the residence of the local station-master of the New Haven railroad. Hadley rented the house for a year and the following spring sold his Hudson River house, which he called Fort William, and bought the house in Southport. For a number of years, after he sold the Southport house, he had a winter retreat in Naples, Florida. He eventually sold the Naples house and for a brief time he had only his apartment in New York City. This did not last long.

When a suitable house in Southport came on the market, soon after closing Parish-Hadley, Inc., Hadley bought it. He has been well received by the village people. Taking an active role in the community, Hadley organized a fund-raising benefit called "Rooms With A View" for the Southport Congregational Church and takes an active role in the annual garden tour for the support of the local library. In Southport and nearby villages, Hadley has given freely of his time at antiques shows that are

PAGES 230–233
Fort William, Hadley's country
house on the Hudson River

organized to help local charities. In like manner, in New York City, he has taken an active leadership role in the Lenox Hill Neighborhood House and in 1996 he was given the organization's Community Humanitarian Award. In April 1999, he was presented with the Swan Ball Award in his hometown, Nashville, Tennessee. The award is given annually to a person who has distinguished himself in the arts and dedicated time to humanitarian efforts. Ambassador Douglas Dillon and Joseph Hirshhorn are among the recipients of the Swan Ball Award.

Having a garden has always been a priority for Hadley. Speaking fondly of the gardens he has created, he said, "Not too many flowers. A green garden is the most lovely. Maybe a little white but no colors." Once when he was on his hands and knees doing some last-minute painting on his front door, getting his house ready for the Southport House Tour, his neighbor called out, "Oh, Albert, it's so nice to see that you do real work." In amused silence, he wondered if she thought interior design was not real work.

PAGES 234–237
Hadley's house in
Southport, Connecticut

While he did not yet know what course his career would take, he was clear about things that he would not do. In the half century of Hadley's career, the decorating profession had changed. He had very definite ideas about these changes. As the *New York Times* said, "He is politely dismissive of the contemporary design scene." In Hadley's own words, "So many young decorators are trying to reinvent the wheel, and the results are sometimes very dubious. They're striving to do things that have never been done before. Quite often it is done without authority, without knowledge, and without a background in taste. They need to be educated about the past, and they need a richer vocabulary. They're all doing beige rooms. Wherever you look, it's all sand and beige and no color. There's very little individuality."

This is not to say that Hadley doesn't like beige. He does. In fact he says that there isn't any color he dislikes. When Margaret Russell, the

PAGES 238–241
Hadley house in Naples, Florida

PAGES 242–245
Shelburne Museum, Shelburne, Vermont

PAGES 246–249
Residence of Mr. and Mrs. Lawrence Brandt, Washington D.C.

editor of *Elle Decor*, said, in Hadley's presence, "Beige isn't a real color," he retorted, "Beige is atmosphere. It's bisque, it's ivory, it's cream, it's stone, it's toast, it's cappuccino. It's, well, it's magic." He is quick to say that he doesn't like certain color combinations such as turquoise blue with orange.

In 1994, just before Mrs. Parish died, Hadley was interviewed by Charles Bricker at *Elle Decor*. At the time of the interview, Mrs. Parish was seriously ill and Hadley knew that major changes were ahead. In the article he talks about the future of interior design:

First of all, forget grandeur. I don't think it is a quality we want today. Too much of what passes for design now is theater. It's one thing to be eccentric—and by the way, most eccentrics tend to be rather well-educated people—and quite another to be a faddist, by which I mean someone who tries to conjure a totally foreign aesthetic in a misplaced environment, like creating a farmhouse mode in a modern glass building. Interiors would be more successful if the designers were a little less intent

on having a good time. Just because a scheme's wacky and off-the-wall some of the young designers think it is FUN, in big letters, when in fact their very determination to be zany renders the results lifeless. What's missing is restraint and knowledge. What's missing is the Zen of seeing.

If we cannot have connoisseurship in the young decorators, I would settle for a few history lessons. There is so little awareness of classical Greece, the neoclassical period, the eighteenth century, and the first half of the twentieth century. Without a foundation the house will crumble. What I am saying is not to be taken for nostalgia. Nothing is more exciting than the new. While you can build on the past, you can never really return to it.

Good design never changes. As Van Truex said, "Good design is forever." Brunschwig & Fils took Van's words as their business motto. The Greeks formulated the principles of design that have been the basis of our intelligent use of materials. None of these things ever change. Proportion and suitability is what it is all about. Decorating is not about making stage sets, it's not about making pretty pictures for the magazines; it's really about creating a quality of life, a beauty that nourishes the soul. Design is coming to grips with one's real lifestyle, one's real place in the world. Rooms should not be put together for show but to nourish one's well-being.

A lot of people worry about the "wear and tear" on furnishings. I feel its more a matter of people treating the things that surround them with respect. Make your home as comfortable and attractive as possible and then get on with living. There's more to life than decorating. Emily Post

turned out to be my great discovery. Why did I read her? Because she told me what life was like in a civilized society that I wanted to be a part of. Finally, it is all about manners.

On January 3, 2000, Hadley opened his new offices, Albert Hadley, Inc., at 24 East Sixty-fourth Street. Making the move with him was his longtime office manager, Carole Cavaluzzo, and her daughter Nancy Porter, who is his trusted secretary. Nancy has literally been with Hadley since she was a little girl. When she was young, her mother would occasionally bring her to the office. According to Hadley, "Nancy runs my life." Three young decorators, Britton Smith, Harry Heissmann, and Peter Lentz, make up his current design team.

It has always been Hadley's policy to bring in young, talented people, train and teach them, and see them go forward to form their own businesses. Most established decorators and design firms want people with proven track records and experience. Not Albert Hadley. He says, "We tell them from the beginning that they are not here to settle in. They are here to learn and, when it is appropriate, move on. It is an opportunity for them to get started. As they move out to do their own thing, our door is open for new, young talent to come aboard." In remembering his time as a designer at Parish-Hadley, Inc., David Kleinberg said, "It would be easy to say that Albert has been a springboard for most of America's top designers, but he's so much more. He's a trampoline!"

Bunny Williams, another leading American designer who began her career at Parish-Hadley, Inc., calls him "the forerunner of cutting-edge design." She goes on to say: "Albert taught us that the past is the foundation for the present, and creation brings us to the future. Where does the genius of Albert Hadley come from? I have often asked. I think it comes from his youth. He is my Peter Pan who is always young and looking forward. He taught me that the future is as important as the past and it is the modern that keeps interiors fresh and exciting. His combination of the past and the future has made the rooms that he created timeless.

"Along with his creative genius, his strength of character and strong sense of ethics have made a lasting impression on me. Years from now people are going to look back with amazement to this incredible man. He studied every kind of design there is and he is able to work in any idiom—Victorian, Georgian, French, modern, you name it. Most decorators find their niche and stick with it, but not Albert. He also taught me that you can be successful and admired and still be modest. He is an absolute gentleman, beloved by his clients and all of the people who worked for and with him. His patience, his understanding, his modesty, and his strong sense of ethics are an inspiration and set a new bar for the design world."

Recalling her experience as a designer at Parish-Hadley, Inc., Mariette Himes Gomez, like Bunny Williams, also refers to Hadley as a Peter Pan and says he has his own special blend of magic sparkle dust that he dispenses. "With one sprinkle he creates simple beauty, amusement, architecture, charm, perfection, and surprise." William Hodgins also cites Hadley's ability to quietly astonish. "It was in one of the early show houses, and

*Screening room designed for
Mr. and Mrs. James Free,
Washington, D.C.*

Residence of Mr. and Mrs.
Michael Druckman, Sutton
Place, New York City

PAGES 254–257
Nashville, Tennessee townhouse
of Hadley's sister, Betsy

254

everyone was doing very typical done-up New York sitting rooms—you know, lots of upholstery and lamps and fringes and things. Albert's room had white rough-textured walls, a wonderful little stone fireplace, straw matting, a French settee in a brilliant pink-and-vermilion woven cotton, a small tea table, a plant, and not a whole lot more. Airy and contemporary, it was just delightfully fresh, and unlike what anyone else was doing."

When Wendy Goodman wrote and produced a feature article on Hadley in *Elle Decor*, her opening words were, "If the design world bestowed knighthoods, we'd all be calling him Sir Albert, which he would hate." David Anthony Easton's reflections on his experience as a decorator at Parish-Hadley, Inc., end with an even more noble title. Easton said, "If it were possible in our democratic world, I would give Albert a title: Albert, King of American Decorating. Long may he live!"

The men and women who form the ranks of leading designers and know Hadley as a colleague look to him with the same admiration. Mario Buatta was working in the decorating department of B. Altman & Co. when he met Hadley. The propitious meeting resulted in Buatta attending a Parsons School of Design summer course in England. On his return to New York, Buatta relied on Hadley's advice to get his first job with a top decorator. Describing Hadley's style, Buatta said, "Albert's sense of decoration is modern for all time with an innate sense of architecture and touches of whimsy in every room he decorates." Tom Britt, the celebrated

PAGES 258–261
The New Jersey residence of
Mr. and Mrs. Adam Kalkin

New York designer known for his exuberant decorating and his no-nonsense opinions, said, "Albert's sense of architecture and space is remarkable. It comes from his ability to make those marvelous sketches; in a few quick strokes, he gets down the whole room and he is able to grasp the essence of a space. When Albert zipped up Mrs. Parish's dress it was the biggest explosion in twentieth-century decorating. Together they were the tops and today Albert still is."

Pilar Viladas, the *New York Times* editor who has written often about Hadley's work, said in the Spring 2000 issue of the *Times's Home Design* magazine, "Albert Hadley is the undisputed dean of American decorators, but his New York apartment is ten times fresher than that of your average twenty-nine-year-old upstart. He knows the rules so well that he can break them with aplomb—and without the self-conscious posing that often afflicts the young."

Today when Hadley talks about New York, he describes the city with the same enthusiasm that he had when he came here fifty years ago. "New York is still glamorous. When I arrived here people lived at a slower pace but perhaps they were smarter in their attitudes. Today if one can hold out against being jaded—yes, New York is still glamorous."

There is something careful about Albert Hadley—his understanding of the continuity of space, of architectural design, elegance, and, perhaps most of all, his absolute and utterly unaffected self-assurance. On his ever-changing, now famous bulletin board, where he puts things that catch his fancy, one finds words and images that subtly reveal the nature of Albert Hadley. He recently added something to the bulletin board that gives a clear understanding of the course he is on today. It is a small slip of paper that says simply, "Catch the wave of the future."

Catalogue Raisonné

Books

Aves, Pirrie B., et al. *Best from the Interior Design Magazine Hall of Fame*. Grand Rapids, MI: Vitae Publications, 1992.

Bartlett, Apple and Susan Bartlett Crater. *Sister: The Life of Legendary American Interior Decorator Mrs. Henry Parish II*. New York: St. Martin's Press, 2000.

Bradbury, Dominic. *American Designers' Houses*. New York: Vendome Press, 2004.

Brown, Erica; introduction by Paul Goldberger. *Interior Views: Design at Its Best*. New York: Viking Press, 1980.

Brown, Erica, preface by Walter Hoving. *Sixty Years of Interior Design: The World of McMillen*. New York: Viking Press, 1982.

de Dampierre, Florence. *The Decorator*. New York: Rizzoli, 1989.

de Wolfe, Elsie; introduction by Albert Hadley. *The House in Good Taste*. New York: Rizzoli, 2004.

Esten, John with Rose Bennett Gilbert. *Manhattan Style*. Boston: Little, Brown, 1990.

Fleischmann, Melanie; foreword by Richard Horn. *In the Neo-classic Style: Empire, Biedermeier, and the Contemporary Home*. New York: Thames & Hudson, 1988.

Garrett, Wendell, David Larkin and Michael Webb. *American Home: From Colonial Simplicity to the Modern Adventure*. New York: Universe Publishing, 2001.

Gilliatt, Mary. *Bathrooms*. New York: Viking Press, 1971.

Gray, Susan, ed. *Designers on Designers: The Inspiration Behind Great Interiors*. New York: McGraw-Hill, 2003.

Gregory, Jamee and Charles Davey. *New York Apartments: Private Views*. New York: Rizzoli, 2004.

Gropp, Louis O. *House & Garden Best in Decorating*. New York: Random House, 1987.

Hadley, Albert. *Albert Hadley: Drawings and the Design Process*. New York: New York School of Interior Design, 2004.

Hadley, Albert, Sister Parish and Christopher Petkanas. *Parish-Hadley: Sixty Years of American Design*. New York: Little, Brown, 1995.

Hampton, Mark. *Legendary Decorators of the Twentieth Century*. New York: Doubleday, 1992.

House Beautiful, the Editors. *Lighting: Inspiring Ideas for Lighting Effects, from Simple to Spectacular*. New York: Hearst Books, 2002.

House Beautiful, the Editors. *Sensational Work Spaces*. New York: Hearst Books, 2002.

Jacobson, Stuart E. *Only the Best: A Celebration of Gift Giving in America*. New York: Abrams, 1985.

Lewis, Adam; foreword by Albert Hadley. *Van Day Truex: The Man Who Defined Twentieth-Century Taste and Style*. New York: Viking Studio, 2001.

Madden, Chris Casson; foreword by Mario Buatta. *Interior Visions: Great American Designers and the Showcase House*. New York: Stewart, Tabori & Chang, 1988.

Madden, Chris Casson. *Rooms with a View: Two Decades of Outstanding American Interior Design from the Kips Bay Decorator Show House*. Glen Cove, NY: PBC International, Inc., 1992.

Pool, Mary Jane. *20th Century Decorating, Architecture and Gardens: 80 Years of Ideas and Pleasure from House & Garden*. New York: Holt, Rinehart & Winston, 1980.

Reif, Rita. *Treasure Rooms of America's Mansions, Manors and Houses*. New York: Coward-McCann, Inc., 1970.

Rense, Paige, ed. *American Interiors: Architectural Digest Presents a Decade of Imaginative Residential Design*. Los Angeles: Knapp Press, 1978.

Rense, Paige, ed. *Architectural Digest Designers' Own Homes*. Los Angeles: Knapp Press, 1984.

Skurka, Norma. *The New York Times Book of Interior Design and Decoration*. New York: Quadrangle/The New York Times Book Co., 1976.

Tate, Allen and C. Ray Smith. *Interior Design in the 20th Century*. New York: Harper & Row, 1986.

Trocmé, Suzanne. *Influential Interiors*. New York: Clarkson Potter, 1999.

Weston, Marybeth Little. *Decorating with Plants*. New York: Pantheon Press, 1978.

Magazine Articles

"The AD 100." *Architectural Digest*, September 1995, Vol. 52, 19.
The 100 top interior designers in the USA as chosen by editor Paige Rense.

Alsop, Susan Mary. "Capital Style: Residences of Robert and Oatsie Charles." *Architectural Digest*, July 1985, Vol. 42, No. 7, 48.
Rooms designed by Albert Hadley.

"American Taste Makers." *House Beautiful*, December 1995, Vol. 137, Issue 12, 86.
Presents photographs of rooms decorated by Sister Parish and Albert Hadley. Americana touches in the entrance hall of John Hay Whitney's home; Triumph of Hadley in saving a New Jersey salon from fresh paint; Design for a room that will hold Brooke Astor's three thousand volumes.

Aronson, Steven M. L. "Amazing Gracie Mansion." *Architectural Digest*, November 2003, Vol. 60, No. 11, 258.
Examines the architecture and interior design of the Gracie Mansion in Manhattan, New York City. The 2003 renewal of the 1799 building shows that the dining room remains as it was designed by Albert Hadley in 1982.

Bernier, Rosamond. "Classic Understatement." *House & Garden*, December 1991, Vol. 163, Issue 12, 132.
The residence of Ambassador and Mrs. Henry Grunwald designed by Albert Hadley.

Berthold, Eric. "Portrait of Albert Hadley." *Showhouse Magazine*, presented by the Junior League of Boston, 1995, 9.

Bohlig, Lois and Richard Fitzgerald. "Patchwork Quilting." *House Beautiful*, December 1968, Vol. 110, Issue 12, 92.
Albert Hadley decorating schemes using patchwork patterns.

Boodro, Michael. "Scaled to Perfection." *House & Garden*, February 1988, Vol. 160, Issue 2, 122.
Albert Hadley's house in Southport, Connecticut.

Bricker, Charles and David Seidner. "Albert Hadley Takes on the Future." *Elle Decor*, June–July 1994, Vol. 5, Issue 3, 116.
Interview with interior decorator Albert Hadley. Hadley's views on changes in interior designing.

Burkett, Harriet. "Rosedown." *House & Garden*, January 1964, Vol. 136, Issue 1, 98.
Rosedown Plantation interiors, in St. Francisville, Louisiana, designed by Albert Hadley and Ethel Smith.

Burros, Marian. "Personal Environment." *House Beautiful*, November 1997, Vol. 139, Issue 11, 110.
Vice President Albert Gore's residence in Washington, D.C., as designed by Albert Hadley.

Cantwell, Mary. "Hadley by Hadley." *House & Garden*, November 1995, Vol. 167, No. 11, 161.
Albert Hadley's Hudson River country house, Fort William.

Carlsen, Peter. "Design: Albert Hadley." *Avenue*, November 1979, 81.
Albert Hadley's Manhattan apartment on East Seventy-fourth Street.

Chatfield-Taylor, Joan. "The Beaux Arts on Nob Hill: Old World Inspirations Shape a Classic San Francisco Apartment." *Architectural Digest*, May 1990, Vol. 47, No. 5, 232.
A San Francisco Nob Hill apartment decorated by Albert Hadley and Gary Hager.

Cheever, Susan. "The Collector's House: An Astonishing Addition to Vermont's Shelburne Museum." *Architectural Digest*, December 2001, Vol. 58, No. 12, 92.
Interior design by Albert Hadley.

Colman, David. "The 10 Smartest Desk Solutions." *Elle Decor*, February–March 1996, Vol. 7, Issue 1, 164.
Albert Hadley and Jeffrey Bilhuber examine the merits of various desk designs.

Columbia, David Patrick. "On Their Own Turf." *Quest*, April 2002, Vol. 7, Issue 4, 31.
Albert Hadley's Manhattan apartment. Cover story.

Cooper, Jerry. "A Tribute to Billy Baldwin." *Interior Design*, September 1987, Vol. 58, Issue 9, 123.
Albert Hadley is one of the designers invited by Luten Clarey Stern to design a vignette marking its reintroduction of five Baldwin furniture designs.

Curtis, Charlotte. "Over the Store: Glenn Bernbaum's Apartment over [his] Mortimer's Restaurant." *House & Garden*, June 1986, Vol. 158, Issue 6, 132.

"Decorating with a Green Thumb." *House & Garden*, March 1978, Vol. 150, Issue 3, 130.
The gardens at Albert Hadley's Hudson River country house, Fort William.

"Decorating with Ideas." *Vogue*, November 15, 1961, Vol. 138, Issue 11, 157.
Albert Hadley's ideas about decorating a house for Christmas.

"Dialogue of Decoration." *Vogue*, April 15, 1961, Vol. 137, Issue 4, 109.
Albert Hadley's ideas on color for five different rooms.

Dorian, Donna. "Nashville Classic." *Southern Accents*, July–August 1994, 93.
Albert Hadley's design for a house that had been the residence of his early employer and mentor, A. Herbert Rogers.

Dumas, Dick. "Up the Hudson." *Décoration Internationale*, September 1983, 83.
Albert Hadley's Hudson River country house, Fort William.

"The Easy-going Cosmos of a Star: Behind the Joel Greys' Discreet Brass Doorplate Is an Apartment Filled with All of the Gaiety of a Triumphant Opening Night." *House & Garden*, December 1968, Vol. 110, Issue 12, 80.

Eberstadt, Frederick and Margaret Russell. "À la Grunwald." *Elle Decor*, February–March 1995, Vol. 6, Issue 1, 136.
The home of Louise Grunwald in Southampton, New York, shows the work of architect Michael McCrum and interior designers Albert Hadley and Brian Murphy. Cover story.

Elliott, Osborne. "In the Grand Manner." *Newsweek*, April 27, 1970.
Parish-Hadley, Inc., listed as one of the four New York City decorating firms selected to decorate for the Metropolitan Museum of Art centennial.

"Events." *Design Times*, November–December 1994, Vol. 6, Issue 6, 97.
Albert Hadley works with inner-city children in Bridgeport, Connecticut, to decorate for a fund-raising benefit.

"Fashions in Living." *Vogue*, June 1959, Vol. 133, Issue 10, 120.
Albert Hadley designs rooms for a seaside summer rental, "Summer on a Shoestring."

Fears, Linda. "The Livin' Is Easy." *American Homestyle & Gardening*, May 1999, 74.
Albert Hadley's screen porch in Southport, Connecticut.

Feld, David. "Glory Days in Manhattan: Crisp Glamour Defines a Penthouse above Central Park." *Architectural Digest*, July 1994, Vol. 51, Issue 7, 86.
Apartment decorated by Albert Hadley for Mrs. Nelson Rockefeller.

"Fifth Avenue Aerie above Central Park." *Architectural Digest*, February 2003, Vol. 60, Issue 2, 134.
An apartment designed by Albert Hadley in New York City, showing details of the architectural design and features of the guest room.

Fitzgerald, Richard and Marion Gaugh. "Mood of Sunny Summers Past." *House Beautiful*, April 1969, Vol. 111, Issue 4, 80.
Albert Hadley's barn in Dark Harbor, Maine.

Fleming, John. "The Private Libraries of Two Great Collectors: A Passion for History." *House & Garden*, March 1987, Vol. 159, Issue 3, 120.
Library of Mrs. Charles Engelhard designed by Albert Hadley.

Forsht, J. L. "In Harmony: Unifying Interior and Exterior Design." *Architectural Digest*, June 1982, Vol. 89, Issue 6, 144.
Albert Hadley and architect Romaldo Giurgola design a suburban house north of New York City.

"Friends in High (Society) Places." *New York*, October 11, 1999, Vol. 32, Issue 39, 55.
Profile of Albert Hadley with a picture of him in Mrs. Vincent Astor's library.

"From Sister Parish's Scrapbook." *House & Garden*, October 1974, Vol. 146, Issue 10, 71.
Pictures of Albert Hadley's barn in Dark Harbor, Maine.

Geran, Monica. "The Bank of New York." *Interior Design*, April 1971, Vol. 42, Issue 4, 120.
Rooms designed by Albert Hadley.

"Glistening News: Silver Walls." *House & Garden*, February 1967, Vol. 139, Issue 2, 113.
Albert Hadley's Manhattan apartment.

Goodman, Wendy. "Albert Hadley." *Elle Decor*, August–September 2004, Vol. 15, Issue 5, 82.
Profile of Albert Hadley focusing on his career background; his reputation in the world of design; and his twelve favorite things.

Goodman, Wendy. "Albert 2000." *Elle Decor*, February–March 2000, Vol. 11, Issue 1, 126.
Focuses on the interior decoration of Albert Hadley's residences in New York City and Connecticut.

Goodman, Wendy. "Decorating's Nobility." *Harper's Bazaar*, December 1994, Vol. 127, Issue 3397, 101.
Albert Hadley, featured as the reigning decorator in the United States, talks about the late Sister Parish.

Goodman, Wendy. "The Top 100 Best Architects and Decorators." *New York*, October 14, 2002, Vol. 35, Issue 35, 34.
Albert Hadley listed as one of the elite interior designers in New York City.

Goodman, Wendy and Alexandra Lange. "2000: Rooms to Be Remembered." *New York*, October 11, 1999, Vol. 32, Issue 39, 44.
Albert Hadley and six other influential New York interior designers and architects, and the rooms they picked to epitomize their great work of the century. Thierry Despont; Peter Marino; Mica Ertegun; Mario Buatta; Charles Gwathmey; Albert Hadley; Philip Johnson.

Green, Elaine and Margaret Morse. "A Young Family Loves Color." *House & Garden*, September 1981, Vol. 153, Issue 9, 123.
Interiors of the William Tomiciki residence designed by Albert Hadley.

Griswold, Mac. "An American Classic." *Garden Design*, August–September 1996, 72.
Albert Hadley's garden in Southport, Connecticut.

Gruen, John and Elizabeth Sverb Byron. "Shades of Grey." *Elle Decor*, October–November 1994, Vol. 5, Issue 5, 182.
The Manhattan penthouse of entertainer Joel Grey. Work of designer and horticulturist Tom Pritchard and Albert Hadley.

Grunwald, Louise. "Mr. Hadley Goes to Washington." *House Beautiful*, February 2001, Vol. 143, Issue 2, 78.
Albert Hadley–designed interiors for the residence of Mr. and Mrs. James Free in Washington, D.C.

Guenther, Wallace. "Choice Foil to City Lights: Olympic Towers." *House Beautiful*, October 1975, Vol. 117, Issue 10, 75.
Model rooms designed by Albert Hadley.

Hadley, Albert. "Guest Speaker." *House Beautiful*, May 1982, Vol. 124, Issue 5, 33.

Hadley, Albert. "My New York: High Drama." *Quest*, April 1997, Vol. 2, Issue 4, 43.
Albert Hadley talks about his admiration of the garden at the United Nations.

"Hadley's Eye." *Architectural Digest*, October 1997, Vol. 54, Issue 10, 38.
Albert Hadley in the antiques shop of George Subkoff in Westport, Connecticut.

"Hall of Fame: Albert Hadley." *Interior Design*, December 1986, Vol. 57, 156.
Announcement of Albert Hadley's induction into the Interior Design Hall of Fame.

Halliday, D. "Designer's Choices." *Architectural Digest*, June 1980, Vol. 37, No. 6, 178.
Albert Hadley's ideas on the combining of functional and decorative objects in interior design.

Hampton, Mark. "A Taste for the Unexpected: Albert Hadley's Refined Vision." *Veranda*, September–October 1993, Issue 25, 50.

"HB Lookout: Polishing the Apple of New York's Eye: Gracie Mansion." *House Beautiful*, October 1982, Vol. 124, Issue 10, 31.
Albert Hadley rooms designed for Gracie Mansion.

Hemphill, Christopher. "City and Country: Albert Hadley Creates Two Distinct Decors for the Same Owners." *Architectural Digest*, March 1982, Vol. 39, No. 3, 120.
The Manhattan apartment and New Jersey estate of Mr. and Mrs. Thornton Wilson designed by Albert Hadley.

Hemphill, Christopher. "A Scent of Sun and Flowers." *House & Garden*, September 1985, Vol. 57, Issue 9, 120.
Enid Haupt's Manhattan apartment designed by Albert Hadley.

Henderson, Stephen. "Rising From the Ashes." *House Beautiful*, March 2005, Vol. 147, Issue 3, 81.
Connecticut residence of Mr. and Mrs. Michael Wiener rebuilt after being totally destroyed by fire. Interior design by Albert Hadley and Harry Heissman. The original house had been designed by Albert Hadley and Tice Alexander.

Hewitt, Mark A. "Living with Antiques: The Pavilion, Ticonderoga, New York." *Antiques*, July 1988, Vol. 134, 130.
Interior design by Albert Hadley.

Hofmann, Isabelle. "Das Weisse Haus am Ufer des Hudsons." *Architektur & Wohnen*, July 1985, 9.
Albert Hadley's Hudson River country house, Fort William.

"A House Filled with Color and Handicrafts." *House & Garden*, April 1971, Vol. 143, Issue 4, 103.
Interior design by Albert Hadley.

Hunter, Elizabeth and Carolyn Sollis. "A Decorating Talent Bank." *House Beautiful*, November 1999, Vol. 140, Issue 11, 74.
A directory of the top interior designers in the United States.

Irvine, Chippy. "Decorating with Antiques: Top Designers Speak Their Minds." *Art & Antiques*, February 1987, Vol. 4, 85.
Albert Hadley's opinions on the use of antiques in interior design.

Irvine, Chippy. "Gracie Mansion: New York's Mayoral Manor Gets a Facelift." *Art & Antiques*, January 1990, Vol. 7, 82.
Rooms designed by Albert Hadley.

Keith, Slim. "Lady Keith's New York City Apartment." *House & Garden*, January 1987, Vol. 159, Issue 1, 67.
Albert Hadley works with Lady Keith decorating her Manhattan apartment.

Kirchner, Jill. "The Decorator's Decorator." *American Homestyle & Gardening*, November 1999, 89.
Albert Hadley's house in Southport, Connecticut.

Logan, Joshua. "Nedda and Joshua Logan." *Architectural Digest*, July 1984, Vol. 41, No. 7, 89.
Rooms decorated by Albert Hadley when he worked at McMillen, Inc.

Loos, Ted. "Potomac Revival." *House Beautiful*, November 2003, Vol. 145, Issue 11, 102.
Interior designs by Albert Hadley and Britton Smith for the residence of Mr. and Mrs. Lawrence Brandt in Washington, D.C.

Loos, Ted. "The Royal Albert." *House Beautiful*, June 2003, Vol. 145, Issue 6, 120.
Profile of Albert Hadley.

López-Cordero, Mario. "How to Decorate a Guest Room." *House Beautiful*, May 2004, Vol. 146, Issue 5, 68.
Albert Hadley's advice on decorating a guest room.

Loring, John. "Thirties Transposition: Mrs. Nelson Rockefeller's Manhattan Apartment." *Architectural Digest*, December 1983, Vol. 40, No. 12, 140.
Interior design by Albert Hadley.

Major, David W. "Housebound." *New Jersey Life*, March/April 2002, Vol. 4, No. 2, 86.
Interior designs by Albert Hadley for the residence of Adam Kalkin in Bernardsville, New Jersey.

Mason, Brook S. "Diary of a US Decorator: Albert Hadley: A Return to Elegance and a Hunger for the Familiar." *Art Newspaper*, September 2001, Vol. 12, No. 117, 80.

Mason, Christopher. "Master Class." *New York*, April 12, 2004, Vol. 37, Issue 12, 66.
Albert Hadley's opinion about young designers; his view that design is about discipline and reality, not about fantasy beyond reality.

Mayfield, Mark. "From the Editor." *House Beautiful*, October 2002, Vol. 144, Issue 10, 42.
Editorial emphasizing the importance of Albert Hadley in the annals of interior design.

McDougall, Mary. "Seaside Urbanity: F. Burrall Hoffman Home in Florida." *House & Garden*, December 1983, Vol. 155, Issue 12, 132.
Interior design by Albert Hadley.

McEvoy, Marian. "Playing Favorites: Observations on Designers Part I. " *Veranda*, May–June 2004, Vol. 18, Issue 3, 20.
Interior designs by Albert Hadley for the residence of Mr. and Mrs. James Free in Washington, D.C.

McMillan, Julie Jackson. "It's Very Hard Work." *Design Times*, January–February 1994, Vol. 6, Issue 1, 73.
Profile on Albert Hadley.

Merchandise Mart, Chicago. "Albert Hadley: Recipient of the First Royal Oak Timeless Design Award." *Decorex USA*, 1997.

Michel, Deborah. "Fabric of Their Lives." *House Beautiful*, May 1995, Vol. 137, Issue 5, 69.
Albert Hadley recounts the history of the origin of the custom-printed cottons of Leslie and D. D. Tillett.

Mint Museum of Art, Charlotte, N.C. "Decorating with Albert Hadley." 1993.

"Mirrors: The Gift of Reflection." *House Beautiful*, December 1968, Vol. 110, Issue 12, 78.
Albert Hadley's New York City apartment.

Morrison, Harriet. "The Beautiful Bath." *House Beautiful*, October 1968, Vol. 110, Issue 10, 146.
Albert Hadley–designed bathroom to be used for comfort and relaxation.

Mortimer, Senga. "Jewels of Design." *House Beautiful*, February 2003, Vol. 145, Issue 2, 88.
Albert Hadley–designed setting featured in the tribute to jeweler Fulco Santostefano della Cerda, Duke of Verdura, at Sotheby's auction house.

Mota, Carlos. "Virtual Reality." *New York*, March 25, 1996, Vol. 29, Issue 12, 78.
Albert Hadley experiments with computers in interior design.

Murphy, Wendy. "Design Dialogue—Albert Hadley: The Search for the Right Clue." *Architectural Digest*, November 1984, Vol. 41, No. 11, 98.
Albert Hadley talks about the "curious eye" that is required in decorating.

"New Freedom in Living." *House & Garden*, January 1973, Vol. 145, Issue 1, 62.
Albert Hadley creates an extravagant bathroom for living with personal treasures.

Obolensky, Hélène. "Hillwood et les Tsars." *Vogue Décoration*, April 1987, 108.
Albert Hadley–designed velvet draperies for Hillwood, the residence of Marjorie Merriweather Post in Washington, D.C.

"Opposites with a Mutual Attraction." *House Beautiful*, January 1971, Vol. 113, Issue 1, 50.
Profile of Parish-Hadley, Inc., Albert Hadley, and Mrs. Henry Parish II.

Petkanas, Christopher. "The Dean's Domain." *House Beautiful*, November 1996, Vol. 138, Issue 11, 188.
Albert Hadley's Manhattan apartment.

Petkanas, Christopher. "Giants of Design: Albert Hadley." *House Beautiful*, June 2000, Vol. 142, Issue 6, 41.

Petkanas, Christopher and Scott Frances. "Once More with Feeling." *House Beautiful*, May 1998, Vol. 140, Issue 5, 120.
Albert Hadley interior designs for the Manhattan offices of Parish-Hadley, Inc.

Pidgeon, Pallas. "The Hadley Half of Parish-Hadley." *NFocus Magazine*, April 1994.

Pittel, Christine. "25 Years of Kips Bay." *House Beautiful*, September 1997, Vol. 139, Issue 9, 112.
Albert Hadley–designed room.

Pittel, Christine and Carolyn Englefield. "Albert Hadley's Small-Town Ways." *House Beautiful*, October 1992, Vol. 134, Issue 10, 78.
Albert Hadley's mid-nineteenth-century Italianate Victorian house in Southport, Connecticut.

"Prewar Palace." *House Beautiful*, June 2002, Vol. 144, Issue 6, 96.
Presents the advice of interior designers Charlotte Moss and Albert Hadley on decorating a classic urban living room. Walls; Window dressing; Sofa.

Prisant, Carol. "Behind the Hedge." *House Beautiful*, June 2000, Vol. 142, Issue 6, 134.
Albert Hadley's house in Naples, Florida.

Prisant, Carol. "Forever Albert." *Victoria*, August 2002, Vol. 16, Issue 8, 58.

Pryce-Jones, Alan. "The Triumph of Tradition." *House & Garden*, October 1985, Vol. 157, Issue 10, 129.
Albert Hadley designs comfortable splendor in rooms that might have been conventionally grand.

Reginato, James. "Household Gods, Passing Fancies." *House & Garden*, September 1996, Vol. 165, Issue 9, 194.
The style of designer Albert Hadley and his bulletin board.

Richardson, John. "An American Attitude." *House & Garden*, January 1983, Vol. 155, Issue 1, 82.
Albert Hadley interior designs for the Samuel Reed house.

Richardson, Nancy. "Creating a Mood." *House & Garden*, November 1982, Vol. 154, Issue 11, 26.
Albert Hadley–designed tabletop display for Tiffany & Co.

Ruhling, Nancy. "Rough Ideas." *Quest*, March 2004, Vol. 18, Issue 3, 98.
Albert Hadley sketches.

Rus, Mayer. "Albert Hadley." *Interior Design*, November 1994, Vol. 65, Issue 14, 110.

Russell, Margaret. "Editor's Page." *Elle Decor*, May 2001, Vol. 12, Issue 3, 32.
Albert Hadley quotations on the color beige.

Saeks, Diane Dorrans. "State of the Art: Albert Hadley." *San Francisco Design Center News*, Summer/Fall 2004, 4.

Saltus, Sarah. "Hadley Garden." *Design Times*, July 1995, Vol. 7, Issue 4, 52.
Albert Hadley's garden in Southport, Connecticut.

Saltus, Sarah. "Serenity Amidst Formality and Charm." *Design Times*, September 1995, Vol. 7, Issue 5, 52.
Albert Hadley's garden in Southport, Connecticut.

Saralegui, Alejandro. "When Harry Met Hadley." *House Beautiful*, April 2003, Vol. 145, Issue 4, 70.
Albert Hadley–designed wallpapers and fabrics for Hinson & Co.

Schultz, Frances. "Home Again Family Treasures." *Veranda*, March–April 2001, Issue 61, 198.
Albert Hadley interior designs for Betsy Hadley, his sister, in Nashville, Tennessee.

Seebohm, Caroline. "When Decorators Garden." *House Beautiful*, April 1991, Vol. 133, Issue 4, 64.
Describes how two distinguished interior designers created their own outdoor spaces. Albert Hadley's transformation of his property in Connecticut; William Hodgins and the acre behind his cottage on the North Shore of Boston.

"Setting for a Washington Hostess." *Architectural Digest*, March/April 1975, Vol. 31, No. 5, 68.
Albert Hadley interior designs for the William Cafritz residence in Bethesda, Maryland.

"Shining Lights." *Interior Design*, December 2004, Vol. 75, Issue 15, S11.
Photographs of the interiors of buildings designed by several interior decorators including the library Albert Hadley designed for Mrs. Vincent Astor.

"Showcase." *Design Times*, September–October 1993, Vol. 5, Issue 5, 86.

Albert Hadley–designed room for show house.

Simpson, Jeffrey. "In the Showrooms." *Architectural Digest*, June 2003, Vol. 60, No. 6, 48.

The Albert Hadley Collection designed for Hinson & Co.

"Soft Twentieth-Century Pastels." *House & Garden*, September 1972, Vol. 144, Issue 9, 68.

Albert Hadley–designed interiors for Mrs. Henry Parish II, featuring the batik fabrics of Alan Campbell.

Solomon, Andrew. "Hadley Pure and Simple." *House & Garden*, March 1992, Vol. 164, Issue 3, 148.

Albert Hadley's Manhattan apartment.

Stephens, Suzanne. "Passing the Torchère." *Avenue*, April 1989, 83.

Albert Hadley becomes the head of Parish-Hadley, Inc.

Symmers, Divya. "An Educated Eye." *Westport*, November 1998, 77.

Albert Hadley's house in Southport, Connecticut, and a broad overview of his work. Cover story.

"Timeless Rooms." *House & Garden*, January 1993, Vol. 165, Issue 1, 124.

Formal reception room designed by Albert Hadley.

"Vignettes at Darius." *Interior Design*, October 1993, Vol. 64, Issue 14, 140.

Vignettes created by several interior designers, including Albert Hadley.

Wintour, Anna. "Romantic Classics." *New York*, October 11, 1982, Vol. 15, Issue 41, 41.

Albert Hadley's Manhattan apartment.

Newspaper Articles

"Affordable Ideas from Designers." *The New York Times Magazine*, April 12, 1987, 8.

Fifteen professionals offer straightforward but imaginative ideas about how to brighten up a room or add a touch of elegance inexpensively.

"Albert Hadley Designs New Print Collection." *The Nashville Tennessean*, February 27, 1966.

Barron, James. "Public Lives." *The New York Times*, May 16, 2000, B2.

House Beautiful magazine honors "Giants of Design."

"Comfort's Back in Style." *The New York Times*, September 25, 1966, 320.

The living room of Albert Hadley's New York City apartment.

Cruice, Valerie. "Raising Money in Designer Style." *The New York Times*, October 9, 1994, CN4.

Albert Hadley works with children in Bridgeport, Connecticut, for charity benefit.

Curtis, Charlotte. "The Reticent Designer." *The New York Times*, July 30, 1985, C12.

If Mrs. Henry Parish II is the queen of American interior design, and there are those who insist she is, then her partner, the shy, scholarly Albert Hadley, is the king.

Diamonstein, Barbaralee. "A Private Library." *The New York Times Magazine*, November 16, 1986, 104.

Mrs. Vincent Astor's Park Avenue library.

DiGiacomo, Frank. "Chez Mike Open for Business." *The New York Observer*, February 11, 2002, 1.

Designer Jeffrey Bilhuber's praise for Albert Hadley's work on the original renovation of Gracie Mansion during the Koch administration (1984).

Duka, John. "In Praise of Patterns: Subtle to Striking." *The New York Times*, January 7, 1982, C1.

The awful truth of interior design these days is that many people would prefer a subtly patterned carpet underfoot, a plump three-cushion damask sofa (with arms), and a restful pattern on the walls any day of the week, rather than a room that seems fixed forever in bare, minimalist whiteness.

Duka, John. "The Subtle Touch of Albert Hadley." *The New York Times*, June 29, 1978, C1.

Albert Hadley's Hudson River country house.

"11 Designers Are Honored." *The New York Times*, December 4, 1986, C11.

Albert Hadley inducted into the Interior Design Magazine Hall of Fame.

"A Fabrics House Updates Its Image." *The New York Times*, January 31, 1966, 44.

Albert Hadley designs new line for the fabric house Jofa.

Ferreri, James G. "Designers at Home: Black and White and Red All Over." *Staten Island Advance*, March 25, 2004, 1.

Comprehensive interview with Albert Hadley and observations of his Manhattan apartment.

"Gardens Are Used to Display Outdoor Settings." *The New York Times*, May 25, 1963, 38.

Albert Hadley designs garden ornaments for Old Westbury Gardens on Long Island.

Glueck, Grace. "Folk Art Paradise Springs Back to Life." *The New York Times*, August 29, 2003, E25.

Albert Hadley designs interior for Adam Kalkin's modern addition to the Shelburne Museum (Vermont).

Hadley, Albert. "Shared Experiences." *The New York Times Magazine*, September 22, 1985, 18.

Albert Hadley's ideas on sharing thoughts about decorating.

Hadley, Albert. "Sprucing Up Aging Walls." *The New York Times Magazine*, April 10, 1988, 393.

Advice on the treatment of interior walls.

Hales, Linda. "Down-to-Earth 'Giants.'" *The Washington Post*, May 24, 2003, 2.

Albert Hadley named a "Giant of Design" by *House Beautiful*.

Hamilton, William L. "Mandarins Gather, and Confidence Rules." *The New York Times*, April 24, 1997, C1.

The twenty-fifth anniversary of the Kips Bay Decorator Show House. Pictures of Albert Hadley's room in the first show house and the scheme reworked twenty-five years later.

Hamilton, William L. "Mr. Hadley's Neighborhood." *The New York Times Magazine*, Part 2 Home Design, April 16, 2000, 81.

Some of Albert Hadley's design resources.

Iovine, Julie V. "Albert Hadley Draws the Shades." *The New York Times*, September 30, 1999, F6.

Article announcing the closing of Parish-Hadley, Inc.

Iovine, Julie V. "Oval Office: Room with a Hue." *The New York Times*, January 28, 2001, D16.

Albert Hadley quoted on rugs in the White House.

Liebenson, Bess. "The Enduring Hadley of Parish-Hadley." *The New York Times*, February 4, 1996, CN17.

Louie, Elaine. "Currents: Reinventing Antiques." *The New York Times*, March 24, 1994, C3.

Albert Hadley designs for Baker Furniture.

Louie, Elaine. "Furniture Throws a Romantic Curve." *The New York Times*, April 21, 1994, C1.

Albert Hadley designs for Baker Furniture.

Merris, Mary. "A Top Designer Says You Aren't Really at Home Unless Your Home Is You." *W*, October 4, 1974.

Albert Hadley's opinions on personal environment.

"The Most-Wanted List." *The New York Times*, January 30, 1974.

Albert Hadley featured in a list of the most socially popular New York men.

Nasatir, Judith. "Designing New York: A Century of Evolving Style." *The New York Observer*, *The Home Observer Magazine*, October 1999, 42.

Photographs of three interiors designed by Albert Hadley.

Norwich, William. "Style Diary." *The New York Observer*, October 14, 1996, 44.

Interview with Albert Hadley, his motto: "The chic of suitability."

O'Brien, George. "Backs to the Wall." *The New York Times Magazine*, January 3, 1965, 36.

Albert Hadley is featured in an article on banquettes.

O'Brien, George. "Living Room Unlimited." *The New York Times Magazine*, June 7, 1964, 102.

Featuring Albert Hadley's multifaceted apartment contained within a single room. It is a testimonial to the fact that limited space need not mean limited living. A good deal of the apartment's success comes from treating the bed (one of the hardest things to disguise in one-room living) as a daybed instead of trying to conceal it.

O'Brien, George. "Updated Designs in Needlepoint Use Modern Art as Inspiration." *The New York Times*, January 27, 1965, 30.
Albert Hadley designs window display for Inman Cook's needlepoint firm, Woolworks.

"Other Experts, Other Thoughts." *The New York Times*, October 24, 1991, C6.
Albert Hadley discusses French curtains.

Owens, Mitchell. "Currents: Sic Transit Sister." *The New York Times*, February 22, 1996, C3.
Albert Hadley launches Albert Hadley, Inc.

Reif, Rita. "At Home with the Opinionated, Volatile, Exuberant Joel Greys." *The New York Times*, July 12, 1968, 36.
Albert Hadley designs a Manhattan apartment for the Broadway star Joel Grey and his wife.

Reif, Rita. "The Freedom Quilting Bee: A Cooperative Step Out of Poverty." *The New York Times*, July 9, 1968, 34.
Albert Hadley selects quilted fabrics from a cooperative in Alabama.

Rohrlich, Marianne. "Mr. Hadley's Well-Drawn Life." *The New York Times*, January 27, 2005, F3.
Albert Hadley's book of his original room renderings.

Rohrlich, Marianne. "A Showcase of Ideas Begging to Be Borrowed." *The New York Times*, April 25, 2002, F6.
Albert Hadley featured in the Kips Bay Decorator Show House.

Rogers, Patricia Dane. "Gores Choose a Decorator; the Roots May Be Tennessee, but the Style Is High New York." *The Washington Post*, May 13, 1993, 16.

Schiro, Anne-Marie. "Bringing It All Together in One Room." *The New York Times*, June 28, 1984, C1.
Mortimer's restaurant owner Glenn Bernbaum's one-room apartment designed by Albert Hadley.

Skurka, Norma. "Design: Holiday Tables." *The New York Times Magazine*, December 12, 1976, 130.
Albert Hadley tabletop design.

Skurka, Norma. "Mating of Traditional and Modern: Peaceful Coexistence." *The New York Times Magazine*, Part 2, October 1, 1972, 23.
Albert Hadley's traditional taste merged with the modern architectural design of Edward Knowles.

Skurka, Norma. "A Touch of Worldliness." *The New York Times Magazine*, March 7, 1971, 80.
Mrs. Vincent Astor's apartment.

Slesin, Suzanne. "$5.5 Million Face Lift for Gracie Mansion." *The New York Times*, November 8, 1984, C1.
Albert Hadley leads committee on 1984 renovation of New York mayoral residence, Gracie Mansion.

Slesin, Suzanne. "Rooms that Frame Photos." *The New York Times*, May 17, 1979, C7.
The Light Gallery commissions five design firms to use photographs in interior design.

"Steamy Luxury." *The New York Times*, September 25, 1966, 342.
Elaborate bathroom designed by Albert Hadley.

Trucco, Terry. "Royal House, U.S. Touch." *The New York Times*, April 7, 1988, C1.
The proposed plans for the private residence of the Duke and Duchess of York.

"Vice President's House." *Nashville Banner*, October 8, 1993.

Viladas, Pilar. "Art Decor." *The New York Times Magazine*, June 4, 2000, 73.
Feature on room portraiture.

Viladas, Pilar. "A Fair Likeness." *The New York Times Magazine*, June 4, 2000, 78.
Albert Hadley's early watercolor room sketch.

Viladas, Pilar. "Grey's Anatomy." *The New York Times Magazine*, March 23, 2003, 44.
Joel Grey's apartment, with references to Albert Hadley's original design.

Viladas, Pilar. "How to Hide a House." *The New York Times Magazine*, May 20, 2001, 59.
Feature on Adam Kalkin's New Jersey residence.

Viladas, Pilar. "Larger Than Life." *The New York Times Magazine*, Part 2 Home Design, April 16, 2000, 71.
Tribute to Albert Hadley and other design luminaries.

Vogel, Carol. "Amazing Space." *The New York Times Magazine*, June 11, 1989, 75.
Mrs. Vincent Astor's Park Avenue library.

Vogel, Carol. "Enduring Decor." *The New York Times Magazine*, March 3, 1985, 72.
New York City apartment designed with Gary Hager.

Vogel, Carol. "The Home Team." *The New York Times Magazine*, August 5, 1990, 55.
Long Island house designed by Robert A. M. Stern and Albert Hadley.

Vogel, Carol. "In the Baldwin Tradition." *The New York Times Magazine*, May 3, 1987, 89.
Feature on five interior designers who made room vignettes for the charity event celebrating Billy Baldwin.

Vogel, Carol. "Lasting Style: Albert Hadley's Enduring Design Ideas." *The New York Times Magazine*, Part 2 Home Design, September 21, 1986, 34.
Albert Hadley's Manhattan apartment.

Vogel, Carol. "Playing Favorites." *The New York Times Magazine*, June 9, 1991, 61.
Albert Hadley shares his thoughts about Philip Johnson's Glass House in New Canaan, Connecticut.

Warren, Virginia Lee. "A Dynamic Design Studio in an Old-Fashioned Setting." *The New York Times*, July 2, 1968, 30.
Albert Hadley promotes the fabric and wallpaper firm of his former Parsons colleague A. T. Hannert.

Wedemeyer, Dee. "New Yorkers, etc." *The New York Times*, January 19, 1977, 54.
Albert Hadley inaugurates Lenox Hill Neighborhood House benefit.

Bibliography

Baldwin, William W. *Billy Baldwin Decorates*. New York: Holt, Rinehart and Winston, 1973.

Baldwin, William W. *Billy Baldwin Remembers*. New York: Harcourt Brace Jovanovich, 1974.

Ballard, Bettina. *In My Fashion*. New York: David McKay Company, Inc., 1960.

Battersby, Martin, revised by Philippe Garner. *The Decorative Thirties*. New York: Whitney Library of Design, 1988.

Battersby, Martin, revised by Philippe Garner. *The Decorative Twenties*. New York: Whitney Library of Design, 1988.

Beaton, Cecil. *The Glass of Fashion*. Garden City, New York: Doubleday, 1954.

Becker, Robert. *Nancy Lancaster: Her Life, Her World, Her Art*. New York: Alfred A. Knopf, 1996.

Bemelmans, Ludwig. *To the One I Love the Best: Episodes from the Life of Lady Mendl*. New York: Viking, 1955.

Bernier, Georges and Rosamond, eds. *European Decoration: Creative Contemporary Interiors*. New York: William Morrow, 1969.

Campbell, Nina and Caroline Seebohm. *Elsie de Wolfe: A Decorative Life*. New York: Clarkson N. Potter, 1992.

Castle, Charles. *Oliver Messel*. London: Thames and Hudson, 1986.

Chanaux, Adolfe. *Jean-Michel Frank*. Paris: Éditions du Regard, 1997.

Charles-Roux, Edmonde. *Chanel and Her World*. New York: Vendome, 1981.

Core, Philip. *The Original Eye: Arbiters of Twentieth-Century Taste*. London: Quartet Books, 1984.

Cowles, Fleur, ed. *The Best of Flair*. New York: HarperCollins, 1996.

Fisher, Richard B. *Syrie Maugham*. London: Duckworth, 1978.

Goodnow, Ruby Ross and Rayne Adams. *The Honest House*. New York: Century, 1914.

Julbez, José M. Buendia, et al. *The Life and Work of Luis Barragán*. New York: Rizzoli, 1997.

Lawford, Valentine. *Vogue's Book of Houses, Gardens, People*. New York: Viking, 1968.

Lewis, Adam. *Van Day Truex: The Man Who Defined Twentieth-Century Taste and Style*. New York: Viking Studio, 2001.

Lewis, Hilary and John O'Connor. *Philip Johnson: The Architect in His Own Words*. New York: Rizzoli, 1994.

McClelland, Nancy. *The Practical Book of Decorative Wall-Treatments*. Philadelphia and London: JB Lippincott Company, 1926.

Morris, Jan. *Manhattan '45*. New York: Oxford, 1987.

Parsons, Frank Alvah. *Interior Decoration, Its Principles and Practice*. New York: Doubleday, 1915.

Post, Emily. *Etiquette in Society, in Business, in Politics and at Home*. New York: Funk & Wagnalls Company, 1922.

Robsjohn-Gibbings, T. H. *Homes of the Brave*. New York: Knopf, 1954.

Robsjohn-Gibbings, T. H. and Carlton W. Pullin. *Furniture of Classical Greece*. New York: Knopf, 1963.

Siza, Alvaro, et al. *Barragan: The Complete Works*. New York: Princeton Architectural Press, 1996.

Smith, Jane S. *Elsie de Wolfe: A Life in the High Style*. Boston: Athenæum, 1982.

Truex, Van Day. *Interiors, Character and Color*. Los Angeles: Knapp, 1980.

Varney, Carleton. *The Draper Touch: The High Life & High Style of Dorothy Draper*. New York: Prentice Hall, 1988.

Vickers, Hugo. *Cecil Beaton*. Boston: Little, Brown, 1985.

Vickers, Hugo. *The Private World of the Duke and Duchess of Windsor*. London: Harrods, 1995.

Vreeland, Diana. *Allure*. Garden City, N.Y.: Doubleday, 1980.

Vreeland, Diana. *D.V.* New York: Knopf, 1984.

Wallach, Janet. *Chanel: Her Style and Her Life*. New York: Doubleday, 1998.

Wharton, Edith and Ogden Codman, Jr. *The Decoration of Houses*. New York: Norton, 1978.

White, Palmer. *Elsa Schiaparelli*. New York: Rizzoli, 1986.

Index

Page numbers in *italics* refer to illustrations.

A

Albert Hadley, Inc., 16, 69, 250
A. Schneller and Sons, 203–4
Astaire, Adele, 43–44
Astor, Brooke, 99, 101–2, 131, 147–76, *152, 155, 157, 159*
Astor, Caroline Schermerhorn, 152
Astor, Vincent, 152, 155, *160*, 164–76

B

Balanchine, George, 89
Baldwin, Billy, 8, 14, 46, 47, *47*, 62, 66, 68, 89, 92, 104
Ball, Peter, *63*, 66
Banker, Pamela, 213
Bank of New York, *178*, 204
Barragán, Luis, 104–5
Beaton, Cecil, 152
Bennison, Geoffrey, 165–70
Bisgood, Allison, 92
Bobrinskoy, Count and Countess Nicholas, 203
Boscobel, 77
Brandt, Mr. and Mrs. Lawrence, *246–49*
Bricker, Charles, 246
Britt, Tom, 256–58
Broadmoor, 23–24, 25, 28, 29–30
Bronfman, Edgar and Ann, 99–101
Brown, Eleanor (Mrs. Archibald M.), 46–47, 69, 72–73, *73*, 81, 84, 85, 87–88, 92–93, 99, 102–3, 141, 152
Browning, Dominique, 209
Buatta, Mario, 256
Burden, Mr. and Mrs. Carter, 116, *192–3*

C

Campbell, Alan, 16, 105, 159, 160, *189*, 202–3
Caulfield, Harold, 45, 48–49, 57
Cavaluzzo, Carole, 250
Cavendish, Lady, 43–44
Charles, Oatsie, 99, 119
Cisneros, Gustavo, *168–9*
Coolidge, Mrs. Thomas Jefferson, *116–17*
Connolly, Sybil, 109–12
Court, Elaine, 112
Crandall, William, 38
Cumming, Rose, 47–48, *49*, 57, 99, 104

D

Dark Harbor, Maine, 8–9, 102, 212, *229*
Davenport, Natalie, 84, *85, 166–7*
Davis, Mr. and Mrs. Leonard, *120–131*
de Angelis, Guido, 203–4
de la Renta, Annette, 120
de Stijl movement, 67
de Wolfe, Elsie, Lady Mendl, 36, 44, 49, 67, 104, 203, 207

Dillon, Ambassador and Mrs. Douglas, 233 house of, 72–4
Drake, Jamie, 145
Druckman, Mr. and Mrs. Michael, *252*
Duke, Matilda, 44

E

Easton, David Anthony, 256
Elle Décor, 209, 246–50, 256
Engelhard, Mr. and Mrs. Charles, 119, 120

F

Fakes, Grace, 72–73, *75*, 84
Ferncliff, 152
"floating apartment," 99–101
Frank, Jean-Michel, 104, 141, 145
Free, Mr. and Mrs. James, 145, *251*
Friia, Mr. Vincent, *180–4*
Frick Collection, 48
Fuller Building, *196*, 212

G

Giacometti, Alberto and Diego, 141
Gomez, Mariette Himes, 250
Goodman, Wendy, 256
Gore, Vice President and Mrs. Albert, 116, 145–47, *147*
Gracie Mansion, 145, *145*
Greentree, 131, *135*
Greenwood, *135*
Gropp, Lou, 209
Grundy, Lester, 63–64
Grunwald, Ambassador and Mrs. Henry, 116, 119, *119*
Guy, Harold, 57

H

Hadley, Albert Livingston, Jr., *43, 229*
  accolades and awards for, 16, 209, 214, 218, 233, 256, 258
  on art of decorating, 75, 206–9, 246–50
  childhood and schooling of, 20–39, *21, 22, 29*, 44
  client relationships of, 116–76
  country houses of,
    Dark Harbor, ME, *228–9*, 218
    Pocantico, NY, 206, 218, 229, *230–33*
    Southport, CT, 229, *234–7*
    Naples, FL, 229, *238–41*
  craftsmen and suppliers of, 78, 202–9
  drawings and sketches by, *34, 35, 36*, 76, *78, 80, 81, 83, 88*, 100, *100, 101*, 145, *164*, 206, 213, *213*, 258
  fashion designs by, 87, *88*, 89
  first homes of, 22, 23–25, 28–30, 31, *45*
  first NYC trip of, 45–49
  influences on, 38, 39, 42, 45, 46–49, 52–53, 69, 84, 88, 99, 104–5

jobs held by, 37–38, 39, 57, 63–66, 67, 69, 87, 92
  at McMillen, Inc., 72–88, 92–93, *92*, 100, 102, 103, 152, 203, 213–14
  NYC apartments of, 14, *14, 17*, 62–63, *66*, 67–69, 72, 88–92, *222*, 229, 258
  Parish's partnership with, 8, 93, 98–103, *99*, 105–20, *109*, 131–41, 147, 152–59, 165–76, 203, 205, 212, 213, 214, 218, 246, 258
  on Parsons faculty, 57, 62, 63, 66–67, 69, 104, 206
  religion and, 30, 44
  as springboard for young designers, 108, 213, 250–58
  as student at Parsons, 12, 52–57, *57*, 62, *74*, 102, 104, 213
  Truex and, 12, 14, 16, 52–53, 57, 66, 67, 69, 93, 104, 105, 108, 207
  in U.S. Army, 42–45
Hadley, Albert Livingston, Sr., 20–21, 22, 24–25, 28–29, 30–31, *36*, 37
Hadley, Amelia, 20, 31
Hadley, "Betsy," Betty Ann, 28, *29*, 30, *43*, 44, 229, *254*
Hadley, Elizabeth Lois Meguiar, 20–21, *21*, 22, 24–25, 28–30, 37, *37*, 38, *43*, 44, 229
Hadley, Howard, 31
Hadley, John Livingston, 20, 31
Halston, 108, 203
Hampton, Mark, 102, 104, 108, *109, 229*
Harper's Bazaar, 36
Haseley Court, *119*
Haupt, Mrs. Enid, *186*
Hermitage, The, Nashville, TN, 31
Hinson, Harry (Hinson & Co.), 11, 205
Hodgins, William, 105, 108, 113, 250–56
Hoops, Elizabeth, 92
House & Garden, 34, 36, 38, 92, 104, 152, 209
House Beautiful, 13, 38, 212, 213
Hoving, Walter, 14
Hurd, Frances, 46

J

Jackson, President Andrew, 31
John Hay Whitney house, 131–35, *131*
Johnson, Philip, 67

K

Kalkin, Mr. and Mrs. Adam, *258–61*
Kennedy, President and Mrs. John F., 98, 99, 147
Kips Bay Show House, 120, *213*, 214, *214, 216*, 218
Kirstein, Lincoln, 89
Kleinberg, David, 250

L

Lamantia, James Rogers, 48
Lanier, Gladys, 36
Lauder, Estée and Joseph, 113
LeClerq, Tanaquil, 89
Leiber, Judith, *176*, 204
Leonard Davis house, 120–31, *122, 125, 128*
Lillie, Bea, 49
Logan, Josh and Nedda, 84–85, 87, *87*
Lord & Taylor, 46, *46*, 62, 104

M

Mayfield, Mark, 209
McClelland, Nancy, 77–78
McEvoy, Marian, 209
McMillen, Drury, 72
McMillen, Inc., 47, 69, 72–88, 92–93, *92*, 100, 102–3, 152, 203, 213–14
Meguiar, Alexander Franklin, 23–24
Meguiar homestead, *25*
Meguiar, Maggie Hillard, *22*, 23–24, 28, 30,
Meguiar, Mary Hillard, 23, 24, 30, 34
Mendl, Lady Charles, *see* de Wolfe, Elsie
Merrill, Eleanor, 78
Metropolitan Museum of Art, 48, 53, 113, 214
Meyers, Reneé, 87, *194*
"Money Room," *147*
Museum of Modern Art, 48, 53
Museum of Natural History, 53

N

Naval Observatory, 145
Nelson, Richard, 98
New York, N.Y., 36, 63, 67–68, 75, 214, 233, 258
    Hadley's apartments in, 14, *14, 17,* 62–63, *66, 67*–69, 72, *222,* 229, 258
    Hadley's first trip to, 45–49
New York Times, 13, 92, 152, 209, 212, 234, 258
Newsom, Lisa, 209
Norwich, Billy, 209
Novogrod, Nancy, 104, 209

O

Odom, William, 62, 72
O'Herron, Mr. and Mrs. Edward, *172–5*

P

Pahlmann, William, 38, 42, 45, 46, *46*, 57, 92, 104, 203
Paley, "Babe," Mrs. William, 116, 131, 135, 141, *141*
Paley, William, 141, *141*
Paley apartment, 135, 141, *141*
Parish, Sister, 8, 16, *93*, 98–103, *99, 103,* 109–20, *109,* 131–41, 147, 152–59, 165–76, 203, 205, 212–14, 218, 246, 258
    client relationships of, 116–20
    decorative style of, 99–104
    personality of, 102–3, 105–9
Parish-Hadley, Inc., 8, 16, 98, 103, 104, 108–9, 112, 116, 119, *178, 196,* 204–5, 214, 250, 256
    closing of, 212–13, 229
Parsons School of Design, 46, 47, 49, 72, 93, 256
    Hadley as student at, 12, 52–59, 62, *74*, 102, 104, 213
    Hadley on faculty of, 57, 62, 63, 66–67, 69, 104, 206
Pippin, Wilbur, 72, 88–92, *93*

Pool, Mary Jane, 209
Porter, Nancy, 250
Post, Emily, 36, 248, 250

R

Radziwill, Mr. and Mrs. John, *171*
Reed, Samuel and Annette, 120, *120*
Rense, Paige, 209
Richardson, Nancy, 209
River House, 81, 84–85, 87, *194*
Rockefeller, "Happy," Mrs. Nelson, 116, 141–45
Rockefeller, Sharon, 113
Rodgers, Herbert, 39, *39*, 99
Rosedown Plantation, 74–81, *77, 78, 80, 81, 83,* 93
Rosier, Roslyn, 57, 69
Russell, Margaret, 209, 234, 246

S

St. Regis Hotel, 152
Schiaparelli, Elsa, 28, 38, 49
Shelburne Museum, *243*
Simpson, Babs, 209
Smith, Ethel, 73–77, *76*
Smith, Gregory B., 84
Spasso House, Moscow, Russia, *112*
Spry, Constance, 44
Stephenson, Mr. and Mrs. Garrick, *164*
surrealism, 34

T

Tiffany & Co., 12, 14, 21, 25, 93, 98, 205
Tree of Life design, *62*, 155
Truex, Van Day, 16, *53*, 62, 72, 152, 206, 207, 209, *218, 224,* 248
    Hadley and, 12, 14, 16, 49, 52–53, 57, 66, 67, 69, 93, 104, 105, 108, 207
Turnbull, Daniel and Martha, 74–75, 77

U

Underwood, Catherine, 74–77
Underwood, Milton, 74–76, 80, 93

V

Vaucluse, 20, 31
Victorian style, 9, 30, 135, 250
Viladas, Pilar, 209, 258
Vogue, 34, 36, 38, 92, *94*
Vreeland, Diana, 49, 113, *113,* 207, 212

W

Wallace, Lila Acheson, 77
Warhol, Andy, 89, 108
Watson, Tom and Olive, 112
Wescott, Glenway, 89
Weymouth, Lally, *165*
Wheeler, Monroe, 89
White House, 98, *99, 100, 101,* 147
Whitney, Betsey, *132–33,* 131–35,
Williams, Bunny, 250
Williamsburg Inn (Golden Horseshoe Club), 81–84
Wilson, Thornton, 186, *190*
Windsor, Duke and Duchess of, 119–20
Wintour, Anna, 209
Wood, Ruby Ross, 46, 104
World War II, 42–45, 52

Z

Zaworcki, Andrew, 112
Zina Studios, 203

Photography Credits

COVER	William P. Steele	110-11	Courtesy of Albert Hadley
Title page	Courtesy of Albert Hadley	113	Wilbur Pippin
Dedication		117	Courtesy of Albert Hadley
page	John T. Hill	118	Michael Mundy*
15	John T. Hill	121	Horst / *House & Garden* © 1983
17	John T. Hill		Condé Nast Publications Inc.
21	Courtesy of Albert Hadley	123	John M. Hall
22	Courtesy of Albert Hadley	124	John M. Hall
25	Courtesy of Albert Hadley	125	John M. Hall
29	Courtesy of Albert Hadley	126-7	John M. Hall
32	Collection of Betsy Hadley	128	John M. Hall
33	Collection of Betsy Hadley	129	John M. Hall
34	Courtesy of Albert Hadley	130	Courtesy of Albert Hadley
35	Courtesy of Albert Hadley	132-3	William P. Steele
36	Courtesy of Albert Hadley	134	William P. Steele
37	Courtesy of Albert Hadley	136-7	Oberto Gili
39	Courtesy of Albert Hadley	138-9	William P. Steele
43	Courtesy of Albert Hadley	140	William P. Steele
45	Courtesy of Albert Hadley	142-3	William P. Steele
46	Wilbur Pippin	144	Courtesy of Albert Hadley
47	Wilbur Pippin	146	Oberto Gili
49	Wilbur Pippin	147	Oberto Gili
53	Wilbur Pippin	148	Oberto Gili
54–5	Courtesy of Albert Hadley	149	Oberto Gili
56	Courtesy of Albert Hadley	150-1	Oberto Gili
58–9	Courtesy of Albert Hadley	153	William P. Steele
63	Courtesy of Albert Hadley	154	William P. Steele
64–5	Courtesy of Albert Hadley	156	William P. Steele
73	Wilbur Pippin	158	William P. Steele
74	Courtesy of Albert Hadley	160	Courtesy of Albert Hadley
75	Courtesy of Albert Hadley	161	William P. Steele
76	Courtesy of Albert Hadley	162	William P. Steele
77	Courtesy of Albert Hadley	163	William P. Steele
78	Courtesy of Albert Hadley	164	Courtesy of Albert Hadley
79	Courtesy of Albert Hadley	165	Courtesy of Albert Hadley
80	Top: courtesy of Albert Hadley	166-7	Courtesy of Albert Hadley
80	Tom Leonard / *House & Garden*	168–9	Tom Feliciano*
	© 1964 Condé Nast Publications Inc.	171	John M. Hall
81	Top: courtesy of Albert Hadley	172-3	Philip H. Ennis
81	Tom Leonard / *House & Garden*	174–5	Philip H. Ennis
	© 1964 Condé Nast Publications Inc.	177	Andrew Bordwin
82	Paul Rocheleau	178	Philip Walton
83	Courtesy of Albert Hadley	179	Tom Weir
85	Wilbur Pippin	180	Mary E. Nichols**
86	Collection of McMillen Inc.	181	Mary E. Nichols**
88	Courtesy of Albert Hadley	182	Mary E. Nichols**
89	Courtesy of Albert Hadley	183	Mary E. Nichols**
90-1	Courtesy of Albert Hadley	184	Mary E. Nichols**
93	Wilbur Pippin	184	Mary E. Nichols**
94	Ernst Beadle / *Vogue* © 1959 Condé	186	Karen Radkai
	Nast Publications Inc.	187	Jaime Ardiles-Arce**
95	Ernst Beadle / *Vogue* © 1959 Condé	188	Courtesy of Albert Hadley
	Nast Publications Inc.	189	Courtesy of Albert Hadley
99	Courtesy of Albert Hadley	190-1	Jaime Ardiles-Arce**
100	Courtesy of Albert Hadley	192-3	Courtesy of Albert Hadley
101	Courtesy of Albert Hadley	194	John M. Hall
103	Wilbur Pippin	195	John M. Hall
104	John M. Hall	196	Courtesy of Albert Hadley
106-7	John M. Hall	197	Courtesy of Albert Hadley
109	Courtesy of Albert Hadley	198–9	Scott Frances

213	Courtesy of Albert Hadley
214	Horst / *House & Garden* © 1974
	Condé Nast Publications Inc.
215	Thibault Jeanson
216	Thibault Jeanson
217	Thibault Jeanson
218	Antoine Bootz
219	Antoine Bootz
220-1	Phillip H. Ennis
222	Dennis Krukowski
223	Dennis Krukowski
224	John T. Hill
225	John T. Hill
226	John T. Hill
227	John T. Hill
228	Courtesy of Albert Hadley
229	Courtesy of Duane Hampton
230	William P. Steele*
231	William P. Steele
232	William P. Steele
233	William P. Steele
234	Simon Watson
235	Tim Lee
236	Fernando Bengoechea / *Beateworks*
237	Simon Watson
238	Fernando Bengoechea / *Beateworks*
239	Fernando Bengoechea / *Beateworks*
240	Fernando Bengoechea / *Beateworks*
241	Fernando Bengoechea / *Beateworks*
242	Peter Aaron / *Architectural Digest*
	© 2001 Condé Nast Publications Inc.
243	Peter Aaron / *Architectural Digest*
	© 2001 Condé Nast Publications Inc.
244–5	Peter Aaron / *Architectural Digest*
	© 2001 Condé Nast Publications Inc.
246	Simon Upton
247	Simon Upton
248	Simon Upton
249	Simon Upton
251	Fernando Bengoechea / *Beateworks*
252	Fernando Bengoechea / *Beateworks*
253	Fernando Bengoechea / *Beateworks*
254	Top: courtesy of Albert Hadley
254	Peter Margonelli
255	Peter Margonelli
256	Peter Margonelli
257	Peter Margonelli
258	Peter Aaron/Esto
259	Peter Aaron/Esto
260-1	Peter Aaron/Esto
272	Courtesy of Albert Hadley
Flap AH	William Waldron
Flap AL	John T. Hill

*Originally published in *House & Garden*
**Originally published in *Architectural Digest*

Drawing room designed for Mr. and Mrs. Stanley Mortimer

Adam Lewis is an interior designer and author of *Van Day Truex: The Man Who Defined Twentieth-Century Taste and Style*. His writings have appeared in such publications as *Architectural Digest* and *House & Garden*. He has lectured throughout the United States on architecture and the decorative arts, studied at the Parsons School of Design and is a graduate of the Yale School of Art and Architecture. He lives in New York City and Bridgehampton, New York.